THE
ANIMAL
BOOK

First published in 2015 by
Miles Kelly Publishing Ltd
Harding's Barn, Bardfield End Green,
Thaxted, Essex, CM6 3PX, UK

10 9 8 7 6 5 4 3 2 1

Publishing Director Belinda Gallagher
Creative Director Jo Cowan
Managing Editor Amanda Askew
Managing Designer Simon Lee

Senior Editors Rosie Neave, Carly Blake,
Claire Philip
Assistant Editors Amy Johnson, Lauren White
Designers Simon Lee (cover), D&A Design,
Rocket Design
Proofreaders Carly Blake, Fran Bromage
Image Manager Liberty Newton
Production Elizabeth Collins, Caroline Kelly
Reprographics Stephan Davis,
Jennifer Cozens, Thom Allaway

ISBN 978-1-78209-892-8

Printed in China

British Library Cataloging-in-Publication Data
A catalog record for this book is available
from the British Library

Made with paper from a sustainable forest

www.mileskelly.net
info@mileskelly.net

THE
ANIMAL
BOOK

Contributors

Camilla de la Bédoyère

Steve Parker

John Farndon

Miles
KeLLy

Contents

Prehistoric GIANTS

Prepare to meet the mega monsters that have ruled our planet throughout its history, in pages packed with supersized teeth, tails, jaws, and claws.

◄ No other meat-eating dinosaur—or any other land-based carnivore found so far—is as big as *Spinosaurus*. This predator lived 100–95 mya, and had long, bony rods sticking up from its back that may have held up a "sail" of skin.

Creatures of THE DEEP

Over 3,000 mya (million years ago), the life-forms in Earth's oceans were tiny, minute specks. But once evolution began, there was no holding back in the bigger-is-better race for survival. From about 450 mya, the first marine mega-monsters prowled the seas.

▼ *Jaekelopterus'* total size is estimated from its immense fossil claw, unearthed in Germany in 2007. It may have been used to hunt prey, as shown here.

Super sea scorpions

Today's scorpions mostly live in desert habitats and rarely exceed 6 in (15 cm) long. In the Devonian Period (419–359 mya), sea scorpions, known as eurypterids, were almost 30 times bigger. *Jaekelopterus'* body length was over 8 ft (2.5 m) and its pincers extended another 3 ft (90 cm). Early eurypterids dwelled in salty water, although later they moved into freshwater. They belonged to the arachnid group, but are more closely related to modern horseshoe crabs.

▼ The modern giant clam is a wanderer—but only when it is a young, tiny form called a larva. Once it settles onto a sunlit spot in the reef shallows, it is fixed in place and grows to be enormous.

AT ALMOST 20 IN (51 CM), JAEKELOPTERUS' FOSSIL CLAW IS LONGER THAN YOUR FOREARM AND HAND.

GIANT SHELLFISH

At 4.2 ft (1.3 m) in length, the giant clam is today's biggest shellfish, but it is tiny compared to its massive prehistoric relation, *Platyceramus*. At 10 ft (3 m) across, this ancient giant's shell was nearly three times wider than the current record holder. *Platyceramus'* shell was thinner and more fragile than a giant clam's, though, so it probably weighed less.

▼ The ancient ammonoid *Parapuzosia* probably had 8–10 tentacles, each one longer than a child's arm.

Amazing ammonoid

Relatives of octopus and squid, ammonoids had big eyes and snaking tentacles to snare prey. Most kinds were hardly larger than your hand. But *Parapuzosia*, one of the last to evolve, was more than 10 ft (3 m) across. It weighed more than a family car at over 1.6 tons (1.4 tonnes), half of which was accounted for by its enormous shell.

Titanic tentacles

Nautiloids were another group of great ocean predators. They were similar to ammonoids but had straight, tapering shells, shaped like a giant ice-cream cone. *Cameroceras*, which lived during the Ordovician Period, 485–443 mya, was one of the biggest nautiloids, with a shell reaching 20 ft (6 m) long. It had beachball-sized eyes and its menacing 7-ft- (2-m-) tentacles could overwhelm almost any prey of its time.

▶ *Cameroceras'* shell was as long as today's great white shark.

Deep-sea gigantism

Today, the biggest living invertebrates (animals without backbones) are the aptly named colossal and giant squid. They live in the deep ocean. Biologists have noted that animals that live far below the ocean's surface are often enormous. *Tusoteuthis longa*, a giant squid that lived in the Cretaceous Period (145–66 mya), was just as massive, at around 36 ft (11 m), including its tentacles.

▶ Giant squid are today's monsters of the deep. Their muscular tentacles are equipped with giant, toothed suckers, which can grab hold of wriggly prey.

BIG Bugs

NAME: *Arthropleura*
LIVED: 300 mya
SIZE: Total length over 8 ft (2.5 m)
DIET: Despite its fearsome looks, *Arthropleura* most likely ate plant matter
HABITAT: Among leaves, fern fronds, and decaying debris on the floor of Carboniferous "coal forests"

Life on land, as in the sea, started out small. The first insectlike creatures to leave the water, more than 400 mya, could fit into this "o." Over time, size became important for survival. Huge bugs crawled, flew, and glided in steamy Carboniferous forests—ferns, horsetails, and clubmosses. Some of these plants were 200 times taller than their modern descendants.

Many-legged champion

The largest invertebrate ever to walk the planet was *Arthropleura*, a giant relation of modern millipedes. It grew longer than an adult man is tall, and had a helmetlike head even larger than a basketball. This enormous creature had around 30 body segments, each with a tough protective back plate and probably two pairs of legs. These may have allowed it to scuttle quickly across the forest floor.

NAME: *Pulmonoscorpius*
LIVED: 330 mya
SIZE: Head to tail 30 in (76 cm)
DIET: Insects, worms, snails, small amphibians, early reptiles
HABITAT: Drier, higher ground in forests that included treelike plants called scale-trees and ferns

Awesome arachnid

One of the largest-ever land scorpions was *Pulmonoscorpius*. Scaling up from a modern species, its stinger would have been the size of an adult human's hand. Unfortunately its fossils don't show if it had potent venom. Today's smaller scorpions, like the 2–3-in- (5–8-cm-) long death stalker, have very deadly poison. Larger modern species have a milder sting, and use size and power to overcome prey.

Flying giant

Meganeura and *Meganeuropsis* were not true dragonflies—they were close cousins called griffinflies. These two bugs were not only the greatest flying insects, they were the biggest insects ever. Top aerial predator of its age (the Early Permian, 299–271 mya), *Meganeuropsis* swooped on plant-sucking bugs called palaeodictyoptera that were themselves very large, with wings 20 in (51 cm) from tip to tip.

NAME: *Meganeuropsis*
LIVED: 290 mya
SIZE: Head-body length 18 in (46 cm), with four vast wings spanning almost 30 in (76 cm)
DIET: Plant-sucking bugs, cockroaches, other early flying insects
HABITAT: Open forests of giant clubmosses, and horsetails as the climate dried in the Early Permian

LIFE-GIVING OXYGEN

Enormous creepy-crawlies lived during the Carboniferous Period, 359–299 mya. At this time, oxygen levels were far higher than they are today—possibly over 30 percent, compared to 21 percent today. Modern insects take in life-giving oxygen along body tubes called trachea so air seeps naturally in and out of their bodies, rather than being "breathed in." The rich air during the Carboniferous Period would have delivered plentiful oxygen along their lengthier trachea. This may explain why ancient bugs were bigger than their modern equivalents.

NAME: *Euphoberia*
LIVED: 290 mya
SIZE: Between 12 in (30 cm) and 3 ft (90 cm)
DIET: Insects, worms, mollusks, small amphibians, early reptiles
HABITAT: Drier hummocks (low mounds) in post-Carboniferous coal swamps

What a lot of legs!

Perhaps the biggest-ever centipede was *Euphoberia*. But it is difficult to know for sure—its fossils are not complete or detailed enough for us to know if it was a true centipede, or a millipede, or some other massive creepy-crawly. Some fossils are only 12 in (30 cm) long, but these remains may be of youngsters that would have grown to be three times longer.

FANTASTIC FISH

The mighty whale shark is the biggest fish alive today—it maxes out at around 40 ft (12 m) and 20 tons (18 tonnes). The great white shark is the most massive predatory fish of all, at 20 ft (6 m) and 2 tons (1.8 tonnes). But prehistory did better—Earth's ancient seas were once home to some even more enormous fish.

ANCIENT SEA ZONE →

Toothy terror

Dunkleosteus belonged to the placoderm, or "plated-skin," fish group. These extinct creatures all had large curved shields on their heads and front ends of their bodies. *Dunkleosteus* was one of the sea's first apex (top) predators among the vertebrates.

▼ The average force of *Dunkleosteus'* jaw is estimated at 5,300 Newtons—slightly more than the crocodile, one of today's strongest snappers.

◀ *Dunkleosteus* was twice the size of a large great white—it could reach 36 ft (11 m) in length, and 4.5 tons (4 tonnes) in weight.

BLADES OF BONE
Dunkleosteus did not have teeth as such. Its jaw bones simply narrowed to thin, sharp blades along its mouth edge. These sliced through almost any victim of its age, even other placoderm fish. *Dunkleosteus* may even have evolved to prey on its relations.

▶ One fossilized *Xiphactinus* showed that its last meal was a fish 6 ft (1.8 m) long—swallowed whole!

Speedy swimmer

Xiphactinus would give the great white shark a terrific battle. This fanged sea monster was 20 ft (6 m) long and related to the bony-tongued fish group, which includes one of the biggest modern freshwater fish, the arapaima. *Xiphactinus* may have had a top speed of 40 mph (64 km/h) so it would easily outswim, and probably outmaneuver the great white's mere 25 mph (40 km/h).

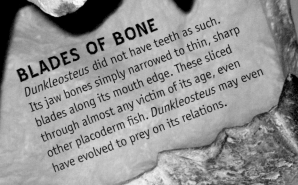

Gentle giant

Leedsichthys is the largest-known fish ever to swim the seas. Its fossil remains have been fragmentary, however, as many parts of its skeleton were made of cartilage, which doesn't preserve as well as bone. In 2013, a research team studied the fossils and declared that the giant fish could reach a maximum length of 52 ft (16 m) and a weight of over 24 tons (22 tonnes). Like the whale shark, its cavernous mouth filtered plankton and other small creatures from the water.

▼ *Leedsichthys'* massive mouth could easily hold 25 bathtubs-full of water.

LEEDSICHTHYS WAS NAMED AFTER BRITISH FOSSIL COLLECTOR ALFRED LEEDS, WHO FIRST FOUND ITS REMAINS IN 1886 NEAR PETERBOROUGH, ENGLAND, U.K.

Over time, larger new teeth were added to the outside of *Helicoprion's* huge tooth whorl, while the older teeth moved to its center.

Spiral saw tooth

For many years, experts were puzzled by strange, circular saw-shaped fossils, some of which were more than 12 in (30 cm) across with over 120 ridges. Finally, in 2013, more fossils and a medical CT scanner study revealed the amazing truth. The "whorl" was actually a serrated tooth set in the lower mouth of a hulking sharklike fish called *Helicoprion*, which means "spiral saw." This creature grew up to 16 ft (5 m) in length.

COLOSSAL Croc!

During the Early Cretaceous Period, 145–100 mya, enormous plant-eating dinosaurs roamed the lands. These giants provided mega meals for their predators, which included other dinosaurs, and also a giant reptile, which lurked in shadowy, shallow swamps—the colossal ancient crocodile, *Sarcosuchus*.

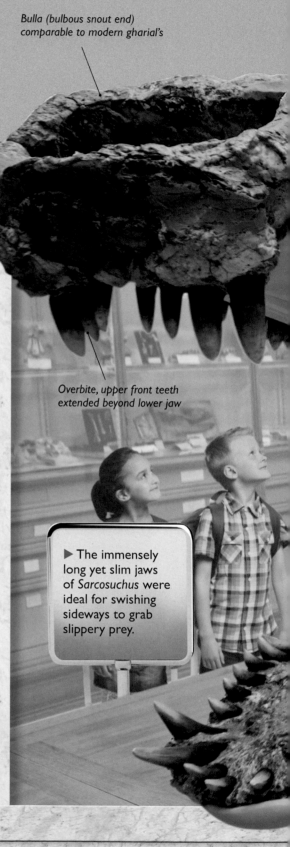

Bulla (bulbous snout end) comparable to modern gharial's

Overbite, upper front teeth extended beyond lower jaw

Swampy Sahara

Today, the Sahara desert is the exact opposite of a great crocodile habitat. But fossils that have been found here from the early Cretaceous Period include fish, amphibians, and other aquatic creatures. There are also remains of plants from river banks, shallow pools, and marshes—and even preserved ripples in sand and mud, showing the direction and speed of water currents. In this ancient mosaic of wetlands, *Sarcosuchus* ruled.

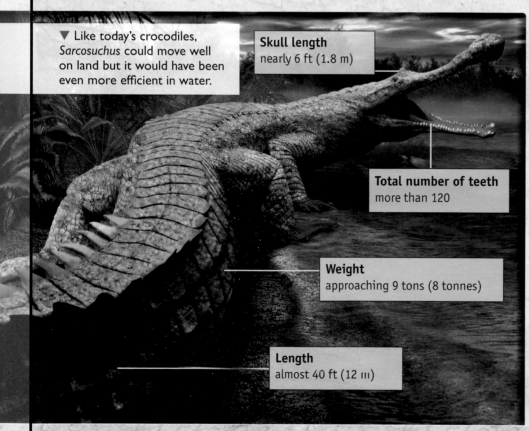

▼ Like today's crocodiles, *Sarcosuchus* could move well on land but it would have been even more efficient in water.

Skull length
nearly 6 ft (1.8 m)

Total number of teeth
more than 120

Weight
approaching 9 tons (8 tonnes)

Length
almost 40 ft (12 m)

▶ The immensely long yet slim jaws of *Sarcosuchus* were ideal for swishing sideways to grab slippery prey.

FOSSIL DISCOVERIES

1867	**1869**	**1907**	**1949, 1950s**	**1957**	**1964**	**1966**	**1977**
Brazil	*USA*	*USA*	*Africa*	*Central Algeria, Southern Tunisia, Northern Niger*	*Northern Niger*	*Paris, France*	*Europe*
Large fossil crocodile teeth found	Crocodile teeth officially named *Crocodylus hartti*	*Crocodylus hartti* reclassified as *Goniopholis hartti*	Various fossil pieces found, possibly crocodilian	Teeth confirmed as crocodilian	Nearly complete fossil skull found	Officially named *Sarcosuchus imperator*	*Goniopholis hartti* fossils reclassified as *Sarcosuchus hartti*

EXPERTS CAN WORK OUT THE AGE OF A CROCODILE BY EXAMINING THE ANNUAL GROWTH RINGS THAT FORM IN THEIR BONES. FOSSILS SHOW THAT *SARCOSUCHUS* LIVED TO AN AGE OF 60-PLUS.

▼ Fossil evidence indicates that the 3-ton- (2.7-tonne-) dinosaur *Ouranosaurus* was a likely feast for *Sarcosuchus*.

Super hunter

Sarcosuchus probably had a similar hunting style to a modern croc, lying still and unnoticed at the water's edge, waiting for its victim to come for a drink. With barely a ripple, it would have silently glided up to its prey, before surging up to bite with ferocious power and dragging down the victim.

Long, slim jaws

Modern giant

On the far eastern edge of the Sahara desert flows the river that gives its name to the second-hugest living reptile—the Nile crocodile. At 20 ft (6 m) long it is only half the length of *Sarcosuchus*. It weighs one ton, and is by far the biggest predator on the African continent, capable of grabbing and drowning any zebra, buffalo, or even young elephant that comes close. It is also the suspected killer of more than 200 humans every year— imagine how deadly *Sarcosuchus* would have been!

◀ The Nile crocodile surges up to leap almost out the water—not even birds are safe.

1997
Niger
Bigger, better fossils of *Sarcosuchus imperator* unearthed

15

King
Carnivores

*T*yrannosaurus rex** was thought to be the greatest land predator for almost a century, and is one of the most famous dinosaurs of all time. But in recent years other mega contenders have been discovered. Larger carnivorous dinos from the Cretaceous Period (145–66 mya) are now claiming the title.

Tyrannosaurus rex
Length: 40 ft (12.2 m)
Weight: 7.5 tons (6.8 tonnes)
Lived: 66 million years ago

Giganotosaurus
Length: 43 ft (13.1 m)
Weight: 8.2 tons (7.4 tonnes)
Lived: 97 million years ago

Deposed king lizard

T rex received its now world-famous name in 1905. There are currently over 30 known specimens, the largest of which is "Sue." This remarkably intact giant fossil was unearthed in South Dakota, U.S., in 1990 and was named after its discoverer, Sue Hendrickson. The teeth of *T rex* are among the longest and probably the strongest of any dinosaur, at up to 9 in (23 cm), curved, and thick.

South America takes over

In 1995, *Giganotosaurus* was named from Argentinian fossils found by mechanic and part-time fossil-hunter Rubén Carolini. This important find deposed *T rex* from its throne. The fossils of *Giganotosaurus* showed it had a long skull, wide gaping mouth, fearsome stabbing teeth, powerful jaw muscles, relatively tiny front arms, and thick, strong back legs and tail.

Spinosaurus
Length: 50 ft (15 m)
Weight: 9 tons (8.1 tonnes)
Lived: 97 million years ago

THE BACK SPINES OF *SPINOSAURUS* WERE UP TO 6 FT (1.8 M) TALL AND ITS SAIL HAD THE AREA OF TWO DOUBLE-BEDS.

Carcharodontosaurus
Length: 42 ft (12.8 m)
Weight: 8.5 tons (7.7 tonnes)
Lived: 93 million years ago

Africa grabs the record

In 1931, fossils found in 1925 in Algeria, North Africa, were renamed *Carcharodontosaurus* by German expert Ernst Stromer, due to similarities between its teeth and those of the great white shark *Carcharodon*. Even larger specimens came to light in Morocco and Niger in the 1990s, and *Carcharodontosaurus* was soon rivaling *Giganotosaurus* for the crown of biggest land predator of all time.

Current king

Spinosaurus fossils were first discovered in Egypt in 1912, but more recent finds in the 1990s–2000s confirmed its status as king carnivore. Further remains of this killer were found across North Africa, from Algeria, Tunisia, and Morocco. The skull of *Spinosaurus* was long and elongated, like a crocodile's snout, with conelike teeth. Fish remains have been found with its fossils, suggesting it also had a diet of scaly prey.

DARKENING the Skies

The biggest-ever flying animals were the great pterosaurs of the Dinosaur Age. Classed as reptiles, they evolved separately to birds. Many were probably furry and warm-blooded too. They were a highly successful animal group, ranging in size from tiny to colossal.

Flying deity

Quetzalcoatlus northropi was named in 1975 after the feathered serpent-god of Central America, Quetzalcoatl. Living 68 mya, its wingspan of 36 ft (11 m) was similar in size to a modern plane capable of carrying four people. Its weight was also extraordinary. At over 440 lb (200 kg) it weighed almost as much as those four passengers. Like other pterosaurs it could flap strongly, but its mammoth bulk meant it probably spent a lot of time soaring in the rising air of updraughts and thermals.

► Like most pterosaurs, *Quetzalcoatlus* had air-filled bones to lighten its vast body and wings.

◄ Two *Tropeognathus* tussle and scrap in midair over a fishy meal.

Snapping jaws

Preserved remains of *Tropeognathus* were uncovered in Brazil's famous Santana Formation rock in South America, in about 1980. It was truly enormous, with a wingspan of 27 ft (8.2 m). Its name means "keel jaw," as it has two strange flanges or keels, like half dinner plates, stuck onto the upper and lower front of the snout. The teeth were pointed and well spaced, ideal for grabbing fish and squid. *Tropeognathus* would have soared and then swooped to skim the sea's surface, dipping its great jaws in to snap and grab its slippery prey.

◄ *Hatzegopteryx* had an immense skull over 8 ft (2.4 m) in length.

Romanian giant

Hatzegopteryx fossils, named in 2002, come from Transylvania in Romania. The remains are scarce, mainly a piece of skull and a humerus (upper-arm bone), but they are definitely pterosaurian. The fossils could be the same as *Quetzalcoatlus*, but they suggest even greater size, with wings spanning an extraordinary 39 ft (12 m). If so, *Hatzegopteryx* would be the greatest flying animal ever. Its name means "Hateg wing" after the region where it was found. *Hatzegopteryx* lived around the same time as *Quetzalcoatlus northropi*, at the end of the Cretaceous Period.

◄ Pterosaur wings were held out by hand and finger bones, especially the extremely elongated fourth finger.

A recent find

Pterosaurs had very light, thin bones that helped their large bodies to fly. This type of bone doesn't fossilize well, however, as fragile bones soon disintegrate. This means pterosaurs are often described from minimal remains. A recent find has been called *Alanqa*. It was named in 2010 from a few pieces of jaw, and one possible neck vertebra (backbone). A very rough wingspan estimate is 20 ft (6 m).

LIVING ON LAND?

Scientists have long puzzled over the lifestyle of giant pterosaurs like *Quetzalcoatlus* and *Hatzegopteryx*. For creatures that apparently spent so much time in the air, their front and rear limbs seemed especially stout and powerful. This led to new ideas about how they lived. They may have spent a lot of time on the ground, walking on their feet and the "knuckles" of their vast wings. In this way the pterosaur may have sauntered with a massive striding gait, pecking up any food it fancied. Then it crouched to spring up on all four limbs, high into the air, with gigantic, dragonlike wingbeats.

OCEAN Hunters

The most monumental predators of the Dinosaur Age (the Mesozoic Era, 252–66 mya) were the marine reptile groups—plesiosaurs, pliosaurs, mosasaurs, and ichthyosaurs. They included some of the largest-ever ocean hunters. The biggest of these species each evolved successful means of hunting and eating prey, in order to reach their impressive size.

Toothless hunter

At 70 ft (21 m) long, and 55 tons (49 tonnes) in weight, the ichthyosaur *Shastasaurus* is the largest marine reptile known from fossils—it was almost great whale-sized. Unusually for an ichthyosaur, its long, slim jaws were toothless. Instead, it probably fed by powerfully sucking in soft-bodied prey such as squid and cuttlefish. Like all marine reptiles it had to surface regularly to breathe air.

✖ SHASTASAURUS

Shastasaurus breathed through two slits just in front of the eyes at the snout base—here closed underwater. This giant lived 210 mya.

KRONOSAURUS

Kronosaurus had an immense head almost 10 ft (3 m) long with jaws that stretched nearly its full length. It lived 115 mya.

Frightful fangs

Of the pliosaurs (short-necked plesiosaurs) known from reasonably plentiful fossils, *Kronosaurus* was one of the biggest. Its frightful teeth measured up to 12 in (30 cm), with about half anchored in the jaw bone. The whole beast had a length of 33 ft (10 m) and weighed up to 17 tons (15 tonnes). Its remains are known from the Southern Hemisphere, mainly Australia and Colombia, South America.

Snake-necked slayer

With a neck that took up half of its total length, experts argue about how the plesiosaur *Elasmosaurus* attacked its prey. An older theory argued it hunted at the water's surface, head held high, ready to dart down like a toothed harpoon to snap up fish from above. Newer ideas portray it lurking below and striking upwards. This ocean killer had a length of 46 ft (14 m) and a weight of around 2.2 tons (2 tonnes).

ELASMOSAURUS

Elasmosaurus probably jabbed at small prey such as fish and squid less than 3 ft (1 m) long. It roamed the seas 80 mya.

A CHANGE IN THINKING

Mosasaurus fossils found in the 1760s were an important trigger for change in scientific thinking. Fossil expert Baron Georges Cuvier (1769–1832) recognized that the *Mosasaurus* remains were from a reptile, not a fish or a whale. This gave him the idea that a species had become extinct. This idea went against the religion-based view of the time, that species were fixed and unchanging. Cuvier adapted his beliefs to say that biblical catastrophes, such as floods, had made ancient animals extinct, then God created a new set. This theory persisted until 1859 when Charles Darwin (1809-1882) published his ideas on evolution by natural selection.

▲ Georges Cuvier changed the scientific view of prehistory by accepting that giant reptiles, massive mammoths, and other species had become extinct.

MOSASAURUS

Long and slim, *Mosasaurus* swam fast by swishing its powerful front flippers and steering with the rear ones. It lived 66 mya.

Late on the scene

One of the last and most deadly of the Dinosaur Age marine giants was *Mosasaurus*. At 56 ft (17 m) long, and with a weight of 16 tons (14.5 tonnes), it was a terror of the Late Mesozoic seas covering Europe and North America. Like *Kronosaurus*, the outsized jaws with rows of robust conical teeth set in the mighty-muscled mouth show that *Mosasaurus* specialized in ripping into big prey.

ULTRA -saurs!

The blue whale wins the title of biggest-ever animal, both today and in prehistory. Incredibly, it weighs in at more than 190 tons (172 tonnes) and can grow to a total length of 100 ft (30 m). The biggest animals to ever walk the land, however, were the supersized sauropod dinosaurs. Working out their dimensions can be problematic though, as often only a few fragments of their remains have been found.

FOSSILS ARE SOLID ROCK—JUST ONE FOSSIL LEG BONE FROM A SAUROPOD CAN WEIGH OVER 10 TONS (9 TONNES)!

ARGENTINA'S CHAMP

Argentinosaurus, from South America, is known from around twenty fossils found during the 1990s. About 11 complete or partial vertebrae, a partial thigh bone, several ribs, and a shin bone were dug up in Nequen Province in West-Central Argentina. From these, experts estimated an upper length of 98 ft (30 m) and a max weight of 93 tons (84 tonnes).

LONG LEGS

With its long front legs and sloping back, North American dinosaur *Brachiosaurus* had a slightly different body shape to most other sauropods. It was named in 1903 from several fossil sets. *Brachiosaurus'* length is estimated at 85 ft (26 m) and its weight is thought to be 38 tons (34 tonnes). The dinosaur had small teeth to rake in large amounts of vegetation.

GIANT CHIEF LIZARD

Another massive sauropod from Argentina, *Futalognkosaurus* was named in 2007 from a reasonable amount of fossil material. Its name means "giant chief lizard" in the language of the local Mapuche people. At an estimated 85 ft (26 m) long and 77 tons (69 tonnes) in weight, it is another contender for the largest dinosaur of the age.

Huge body needed to digest large amounts of plant matter

Long neck allowed easy browsing

Columnlike legs bore hefty weight, perhaps 22 tons (20 tonnes) each

Long, heavy tapering tail

Back slopes down at the rear

Curved head crest

Bony projections (neural spines) along top of neck

Tail held off ground

Greatly elongated neck

Wide-set legs flank huge rib cage

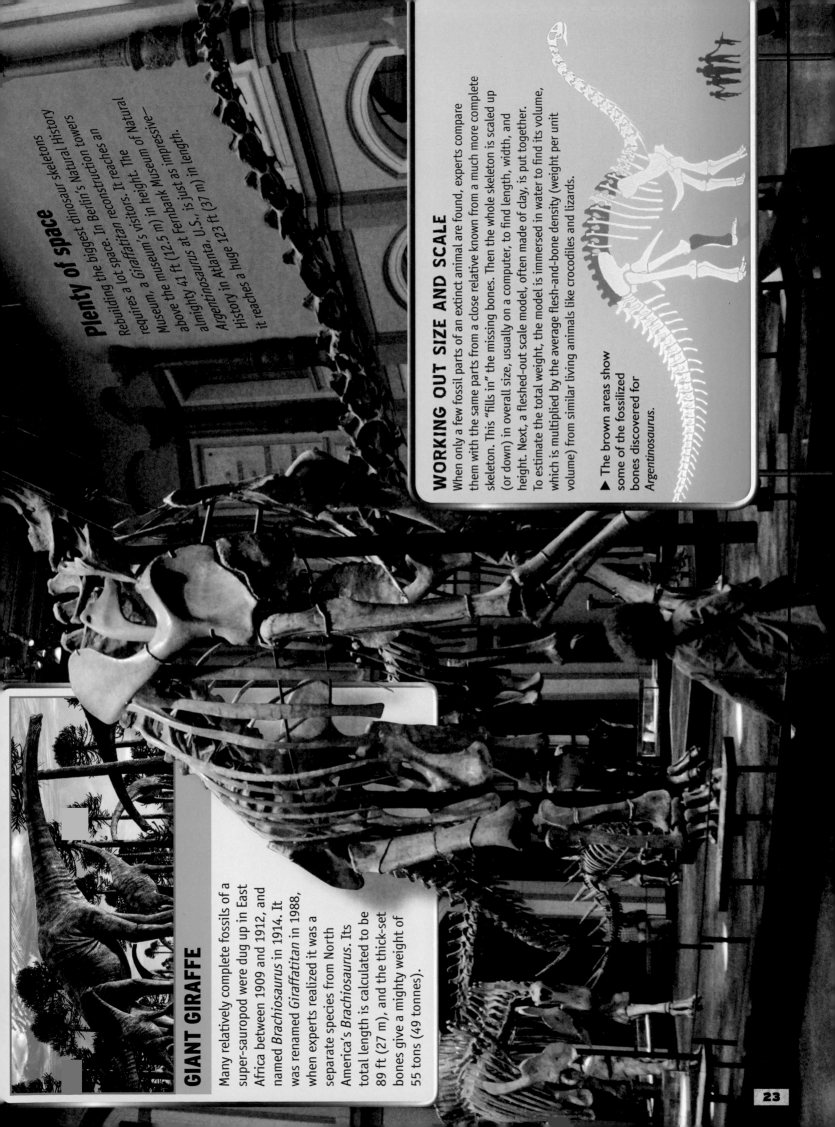

Plenty of space

Rebuilding the biggest dinosaur skeletons requires a lot of space. In Berlin's Natural History Museum, the museum—impressive—Museum of Natural reaches an almighty 41 ft (12.5 m) in height. The requires a *Giraffatitan's* visitors. The reconstruction. It reaches an above the museum—impressive—Museum of Natural reaches an almighty 41 ft (12.5 m) in height. The *Argentinosaurus*, U.S., is just as History in Atlanta 123 ft (37 m) in length. it reaches a huge 123 ft (37 m) in length.

GIANT GIRAFFE

Many relatively complete fossils of a super-sauropod were dug up in East Africa between 1909 and 1912, and named *Brachiosaurus* in 1914. It was renamed *Giraffatitan* in 1988, when experts realized it was a separate species from North America's *Brachiosaurus*. Its total length is calculated to be 89 ft (27 m), and the thick-set bones give a mighty weight of 55 tons (49 tonnes).

WORKING OUT SIZE AND SCALE

When only a few fossil parts of an extinct animal are found, experts compare them with the same parts from a close relative known from a much more complete skeleton. This "fills in" the missing bones. Then the whole skeleton is scaled up (or down) in overall size, usually on a computer, to find length, width, and height. Next, a fleshed-out scale model, often made of clay, is put together. To estimate the total weight, the model is immersed in water to find its volume, which is multiplied by the average flesh-and-bone density (weight per unit volume) from similar living animals like crocodiles and lizards.

▶ The brown areas show some of the fossilized bones discovered for *Argentinosaurus*.

DINO Champions

The mighty dinosaurs were not only record-breakers in size. From the biggest-ever claws to the most mega head crest, these champion reptiles ruled the planet for 150 million years, and exhibited some of the most massive body features imaginable.

▼ In the 1990s, experts worked out what *Therizinosaurus* may have looked like, with its strange mix of features.

Parasaurolophus
Meaning: "Near crested lizard"
Group: Hadrosaurs or "duckbills"
Length: 30 ft (9 m)
Weight: 3 tons (2.7 tonnes)
Head crest: 7 ft (2 m) long

Enormous claws

The biggest claws of any animal ever belong to the therizinosaurs or "scythe-lizards." Their closest cousins were the small, fast, and fierce meat-eating raptors, but the largest kind, *Therizinosaurus*, was as huge as a *Tyrannosaurus*. Its massive claws are only one of its odd features—it had a small head, long neck, and a wide, bulky body. Experts are still unsure why its claws were so enormous—maybe they sliced off or raked up leaves to eat, dug up termites and similar bugs as food, or perhaps their claws were used to fight off predators.

Remarkable crest

On its head, the hadrosaur *Parasaurolophus* had a peculiar long, curved crest that was even longer than a human. Hollow with breathing passages, the crest may have worked as a kind of cooling air-conditioning unit and could also have amplified the dinosaur's honks, roars, or bellows when shaken from side to side. This sound-and-vision display would frighten enemies, threaten herd rivals, and attract breeding mates.

▼ *Parasaurolophus'* crest may have turned a bright color at breeding time, to attract mates.

Therizinosaurus
Meaning: "Reaper/scythe lizard"
Group: therizinosaurs
Length: 36 ft (11 m)
Weight: 6.5 tons (6 tonnes)
Claws: 3 ft (90 cm) long

IN THE 1940S IT WAS THOUGHT THAT *THERIZINOSAURUS* FOSSIL CLAWS CAME FROM A GIANT SEA TURTLE THAT USED THEM TO CHOP SEAWEED!

► Few enemies would take on a herd of charging *Triceratops*, their horns ready to stab and gouge.

Heavy horns

There are hundreds of fossils of *Triceratops* horns—but usually all that remains is the bony part, or core, which grew out of the skull. In life, this bony core was probably covered by a sheath of horny keratin (the fibrous protein that makes up a bird's beak, dinosaur claws, and your fingernails). The keratin sheath would make the horn even longer—and sharper.

Triceratops
Meaning: "Three-horned face"
Group: Ceratopsians
Length: 29 ft (9 m)
Weight: 10 tons (9 tonnes)
Horns: Over 3 ft (90 cm)

MEGA-EGGS

Sometimes eggs form fossils, but it's difficult to know what animal originally laid them. Some eggs that have been discovered are so big—18 in (45 cm) long—that a dinosaur parent seems the obvious answer. The remains were broken, misshapen, and tricky to reconstruct however, so scientists can't be sure.

The longest neck

Most sauropods had long necks but none so lengthy as *Mamenchisaurus sinocanadorum*, discovered in 1993 in southwest China. Its neck was about half its total body length. This immense herbivore may have swung its tiny head from side to side in a vast arc, the neck pivoting mainly near the shoulders, as it plodded along, munching plant food.

► Joints between the long, light cervical vertebrae (neck bones) of *Mamenchisaurus* suggest the middle of the neck was quite stiff.

Mamenchisaurus
Meaning: "Horse-gate stream lizard"
Group: Sauropods
Length: Over 110 ft (33 m)
Weight: 35 tons (31.7 tonnes)
Neck: 55 ft (17 m)

► These fossil eggs are probably from *Titanosaurus*, a huge sauropod dinosaur.

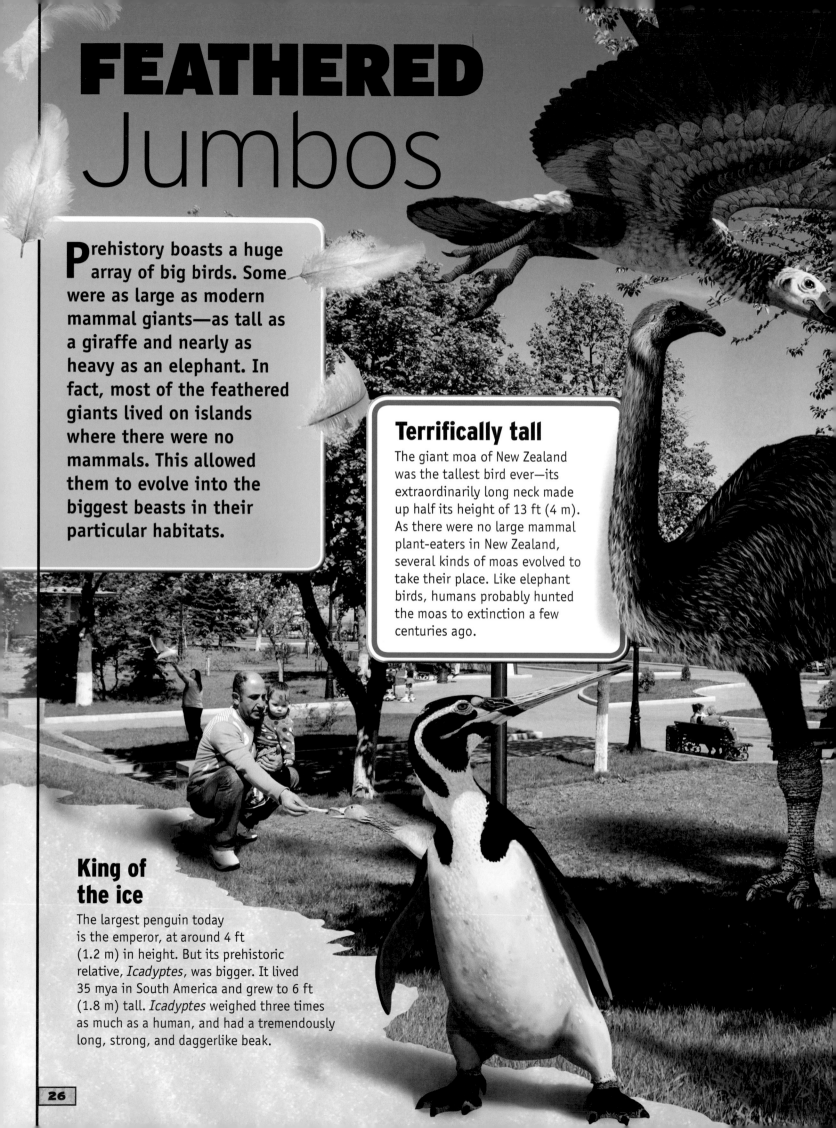

FEATHERED
Jumbos

Prehistory boasts a huge array of big birds. Some were as large as modern mammal giants—as tall as a giraffe and nearly as heavy as an elephant. In fact, most of the feathered giants lived on islands where there were no mammals. This allowed them to evolve into the biggest beasts in their particular habitats.

Terrifically tall

The giant moa of New Zealand was the tallest bird ever—its extraordinarily long neck made up half its height of 13 ft (4 m). As there were no large mammal plant-eaters in New Zealand, several kinds of moas evolved to take their place. Like elephant birds, humans probably hunted the moas to extinction a few centuries ago.

King of the ice

The largest penguin today is the emperor, at around 4 ft (1.2 m) in height. But its prehistoric relative, *Icadyptes*, was bigger. It lived 35 mya in South America and grew to 6 ft (1.8 m) tall. *Icadyptes* weighed three times as much as a human, and had a tremendously long, strong, and daggerlike beak.

Whopping wingspan

Also called the giant teratorn, *Argentavis* is named after the country where its fossils have been found—Argentina, in South America. It looked like a modern vulture but was over twice the size, standing more than 6 ft (1.8 m) tall. It was the biggest ever flying bird, and tore up prey with its deadly hooked beak. Its wingspan reached 23 ft (7 m), and it weighed 155 lb (70 kg).

Humongously heavy

The bulkiest land bird ever to exist was the giant elephant bird *Aepyornis maximus*, weighing in at almost half a ton, and standing 9 ft (2.7 m) tall. It survived until around 400 years ago on the island of Madagascar, in the Indian Ocean. As the bird was so outsized it couldn't fly—or escape its human hunters. They were the likely cause of its extinction—as well as hunting the adults, humans also collected the birds' huge eggs and chicks.

COMPARING EGGS

An elephant bird egg was twice as long and 15 times heavier than today's largest eggs, which come from the ostrich. The prehistoric egg weighed a hefty 50 lb (23 kg), while the modern ostrich egg tips the scales at 3.5 lb (1.6 kg).

MEGA Island

Today, Australia is home to some of the most extraordinary creatures in the animal kingdom—and the same was true in prehistory. This is because the island continent has been isolated for more than 90 million years. Ancient Australian land animals evolved in very different ways to those elsewhere, and the result was a spectacular array of mega-beasts.

River giant

Freshwater turtles today rarely exceed a shell length of 3 ft (90 cm). Australia's great horned turtle, *Meiolania*, was almost three times as long, at over 8 ft (2.4 m), and probably ten times heavier, at 1,550 lb (703 kg). Fossils suggest it could have survived on some islands until just a few centuries ago—millennia after humans hunted it to extinction on the mainland.

▷ *Meiolania* had a thick, domed shell and its legs were probably strong enough to walk on land.

Monster lizard

Less than 50,000 years ago the largest-ever lizard, *Megalania*, prowled Australia. Up to 23 ft (7 m) long and weighing perhaps 1,000 lb (454 kg), it was over twice as long and seven times heavier than today's biggest lizard, and its close relation, the komodo dragon. It had a large skull, a low, wide body, and a long muscular tail. The main fossils of this giant predator are around 30,000 years old.

◁ Scavenging *Megalanias* may have battled over a dead carcass using their great gaping jaws and serrated, back-curved fangs.

AT 7.2 FT (2.2 M) TALL, AND 500 LB (227 KG) IN WEIGHT, THE SHORT-FACED KANGAROO, *PROCOPTODON*, WAS THE BIGGEST-EVER KANGAROO. LIKE SO MANY AUSTRALIAN GIANTS ITS EXTINCTION WAS PROBABLY CAUSED BY HUMANS, AROUND 15,000 YEARS AGO.

Mega biter

The marsupial lion, *Thylacoleo*, was slightly smaller than today's lion, at 6 ft (1.8 m) long and 330 lb (150 kg) in weight. But its bite force is estimated at more than its modern equivalent—perfect for stabbing and crushing the bones of prey, such as the giant short-faced kangaroo.

▼ *Thylacoleo's* thumb claw could deliver a quick slash at prey. The marsupial lion would then retreat while its victim bled to death.

WHAT ARE MARSUPIALS?

Australia is well known for its unique mammals called marsupials. Their babies are born very early in development—tiny, with no fur, and no proper eyes, ears, or limbs. They just manage to crawl to the mother's marsupium (pouch), to continue development.

Thunderbirds

Giant extinct ground birds are known to have lived on many islands. Australia had one—Stirton's thunderbird, or *Dromornis stirtoni*. Only a few fossils are known, but estimates put this enormous, muscular creature at up to 3 m (10 ft) high and weighing 1,000 lb (454 kg). It had powerful legs that enabled it to run, a bulky body, and a strong beak to attack prey.

▲ The enormous Stirton's thunderbird had an almost bathtub-sized bill that could easily pick up and swallow prey, such as joeys (young kangaroos).

Titan SAFARI

What is the biggest land mammal ever to walk planet Earth? A giraffe, a rhino, or an elephant? They are mega, certainly, but not the hugest. The title goes to a cousin of rhinos that lived in several parts of Asia, over 25 mya. It is known by its general name of *Paraceratherium*, most of the time...

Monster mother

Today's rhinos are mostly solitary beasts, mainly living alone apart from a mother with her young, or calf. The calf follows its mother closely for one to two years—and she is one of the fiercest, most protective parents in the animal world. If *Paraceratherium* was similar, few predators would dare to enrage such a massive mother, whose maternal instincts would be to charge at any potential enemy, head-butt it, and trample it into the earth.

Naming the beast

Most experts now call the biggest-ever land mammal *Paraceratherium*, which means "near horn beast." In the past, as new fossils were discovered, experts disagreed about its name and whether the different specimens belonged to the same family. It has been called *Baluchitherium* and *Indricotherium* among others. The argument was put to rest in 1989 when an expert review suggested all the genera should be known as *Paraceratherium*, with about four or five distinct species.

Relatively slim body

▶ *Paraceratherium* traveled to wooded areas to browse for food.

Tall legs for long strides

The biggest of all

Many *Paraceratherium* specimens are known from well-preserved fossils. Working from these, experts can scale up the dimensions for individuals with far fewer, but much larger, remains than these smaller examples. From this, we know that its length could approach 33 ft (10 m), with a shoulder height of up to 18 ft (5.5 m).

▼ *Paraceratherium* would tower over today's biggest land animals.

Height (ft)
20
18
16
14
12
10
8
6
4
2
0

Paraceratherium

African elephant

White rhinoceros

Long, sturdy neck

Long, low skull

Leaf-stripping teeth

Prehensile lips

▼ *Paraceratherium's* long, slim legs made it more energy efficient whilst looking for food.

Why so big?

Over millions of years, a number of evolutionary pressures enabled *Paraceratherium* to become such a blockbuster. Its rhino group heritage gave it a large body size to start with. It is possible that at the time of its existence many other herbivores competed for low-growing vegetation. Higher leaves in trees were relatively unexploited food sources and so over many generations, natural selection favored creatures with longer necks and legs. A greater bulk was also a form of defense against predators.

ANOTHER MONSTER MAMMAL

Many other mammal herbivores evolved to become enormous. For example the "terminator pig" *Daeodon*, which lived in North America 25 mya, could grow to a length of 12 ft (3.6 m) and may have weighed 2,000 lb (907 kg).

▶ *Daeodon* would have been a match for the leading predator of its time, the wolflike creodont *Hyaenodon*.

SUPERSIZED
Serpents

No sooner did the great dinosaurs become extinct at the end of the Cretaceous Period, 66 mya, than new sets of huge land creatures evolved to take their place. These included super-sized snakes and enormous amphibians.

CRUSHING COMPARISONS

The biggest snakes today are the reticulated python at around 30 ft (9 m), and the green anaconda, which reaches 220 lb (100 kg). *Titanoboa*, also in the constricting snake group, would have dwarfed them—it was nearly twice as long and maybe five times as heavy. Its scales could have been the size of your hand.

▼ *Prionosuchus* had a long snout, sharp teeth and an elongated body.

All-conquering amphibian

In South America during the Permian Period (299–252 mya), dwelled the huge *Prionosuchus*. It could have reached 33 ft (10 m) in length, and looked like a mix of crocodile and snake. But it was not a reptile, it was an amphibian—a giant version of today's salamanders, which grow to a maximum of about 5 ft (1.5 m).

Tropical titan

Titanoboa fossils come from Colombia, South America, and date to the post-dinosaur Paleocene Epoch, between 66–56 mya. Other fossils found with it indicate a highly tropical environment where cold-blooded creatures like reptiles were warm enough to move and hunt year-round. The upper estimate for *Titanoboa's* length is an incredible 50 ft (15.2 m).

▼ *Titanoboa* was not only long—it was seriously heavy, at up to 2,000 lb (907 kg).

AMAZINGLY, ONE ENORMOUS VICTIM COULD PROVIDE GIANT SNAKE *TITANOBOA* WITH ENOUGH FOOD FOR AN ENTIRE YEAR.

This fossil-rich rock from around 50 mya contains vertebrae or backbones of *Palaeophis*.

▶ Enormous *Gigantophis* probably grew up to 36 ft (11 m) in length.

More mega constrictors

Two other massive prehistoric snakes were *Palaeophis* and *Gigantophis*. *Gigantophis* is known from fossils found in North Africa. Like *Titanoboa* it was probably a muscular, coiling constrictor. *Palaeophis*, at up to 33 ft (10 m) long, lived in the sea, although it was vastly bigger than any sea snake today. Its fossils come from Europe and North Africa.

The Giants of South America

Just like the marsupial giants of Australia, the extinct heavyweights of South America demonstrate island evolution. The continent has been isolated, on and off, for long periods over the past 220 million years. This resulted in its animals following their own unique lines of evolution.

The famous giant sloth

Megatherium was massive—as big as an elephant. It walked on the sides of its feet because its toes had long, sharp claws. These were probably used for defense and for hooking leaves into its mouth. When its fossils were found in Argentina in the 1770s, people were amazed. In 1796, Georges Cuvier named it Megatherium, meaning simply "mega beast."

▲ Megatherium is related to modern tree sloths, but was far bigger—it grew to 20 ft (6 m) in length and weighed 4.4 tons (4 tonnes).

DARWIN'S IDEAS

The scientist Charles Darwin (1809–1882) changed the way people thought about life on Earth. He argued that over millions of years, animals and plants adapted to Earth's ever-changing environments. If a species was unable to change quickly enough, it would die out. He used fossils as evidence for this theory.

From seeing enormous Megatherium fossils Darwin began to form his evolutionary ideas.

Darwin discovered the first Macrauchenia fossils on the South American plains.

Strange-looking grazer

Macrauchenia looked like a horse and a camel, but in fact it belonged to the hoofed mammal group known as litopterns, which were found only in South America. It was a sizeable creature at 10 ft (3 m) long, making it a great meal for predators such as Smilodon, the saber-toothed cat. Macrauchenia probably evolved to grasp leaves from trees, as it was a browsing herbivore.

▲ Macrauchenia lived in huge herds on the South American plains up until around 20,000 years ago.

The strong beaks of the phorusrhacids could bite and slash victims. These birds were deadly hunters, evolved to kill.

Fossils of Toxodon's skull show it had continuously growing cheek teeth.

Humongous beast

Big and bulky, Toxodon was one of the largest grazers of South America. It looked quite similar to the modern rhino, which evolved separately in North America and Eurasia. Toxodon had an enormous skeleton to support its massive body, and a large shoulder hump.

▼ Toxodon grew to nearly 9 ft (2.7 m) in length, making it similar in size to today's hippopotamus.

Terrifying birds

The phorusrhacids were a group of enormous flightless, meat-eating predators. They were given the nickname "terror birds" due to their ferocious hunting skills. The biggest-known kind was *Kelenken* from Argentina—its hooked beak measured more than 18 in (45 cm) long. It weighed an impressive 500 lb (228 kg) and grew up to 10 ft (3 m) tall.

▼ *Phorusrhacos* was also a member of the "terror bird" group, shown here mid-attack. It reached 8.2 ft (2.5 m) in height.

Enormous armor

Glyptodon looked like a huge armadillo. It ambled along as it chewed plant matter, safe inside the bony armored casing that even covered its head and tail. It weighed a hefty 2.1 tons (1.9 tonnes) and was 11 ft (3.3 m) long— roughly the same size and shape as a small car.

Glyptodon fossils show how the animal's protective casing was made up of lots of small, bony plates.

Doedicurus, a relative of Glyptodon, had a spiked club tail that could weigh as much as an adult man.

MONUMENTAL
Mammoths

Mammoths are the enormous extinct relatives of modern elephants. Their remains have been found in many places around the world, as far south as Mexico and as far north as Alaska. The best remains have been found in Siberia, where bodies have stayed frozen for thousands of years.

A mammoth's enormous tusks could be displayed to rivals and enemies or used as defense against predators. They also swept away snow to allow access to ground and low-growing plant food, and could dig up roots and bulbs.

Epic elephants

The elephant family, Proboscidea, has been around for almost 60 million years. Early members were dog-sized, but they soon evolved huge bodies, tusks, and trunks. These enormous body features provided great power and strength, and as a result, mammoths dominated other plant-eating competitors that might have wanted to muscle in on their food supplies.

The long trunk was used during communication and for eating and drinking.

◀ Male steppe mammoths had tusks that could grow to an incredible 18 ft (5.5 m) in length.

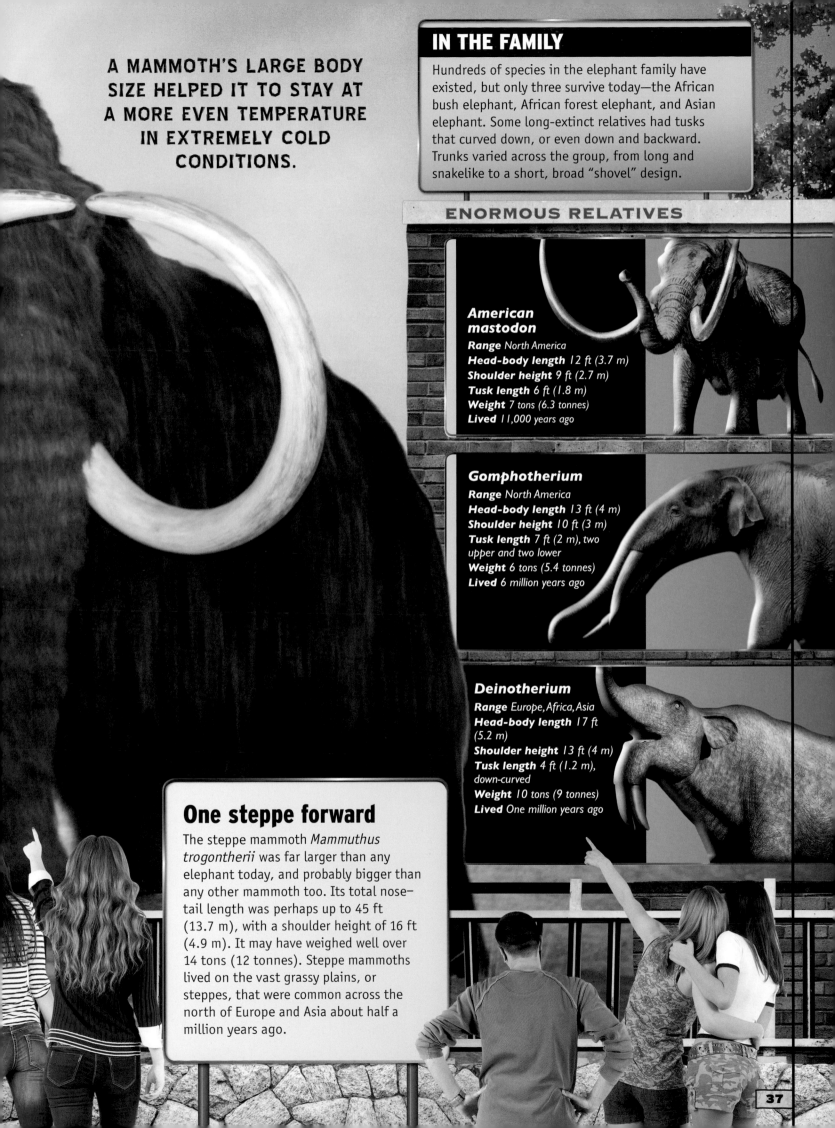

A MAMMOTH'S LARGE BODY SIZE HELPED IT TO STAY AT A MORE EVEN TEMPERATURE IN EXTREMELY COLD CONDITIONS.

IN THE FAMILY

Hundreds of species in the elephant family have existed, but only three survive today—the African bush elephant, African forest elephant, and Asian elephant. Some long-extinct relatives had tusks that curved down, or even down and backward. Trunks varied across the group, from long and snakelike to a short, broad "shovel" design.

ENORMOUS RELATIVES

American mastodon
Range North America
Head-body length 12 ft (3.7 m)
Shoulder height 9 ft (2.7 m)
Tusk length 6 ft (1.8 m)
Weight 7 tons (6.3 tonnes)
Lived 11,000 years ago

Gomphotherium
Range North America
Head-body length 13 ft (4 m)
Shoulder height 10 ft (3 m)
Tusk length 7 ft (2 m), two upper and two lower
Weight 6 tons (5.4 tonnes)
Lived 6 million years ago

Deinotherium
Range Europe, Africa, Asia
Head-body length 17 ft (5.2 m)
Shoulder height 13 ft (4 m)
Tusk length 4 ft (1.2 m), down-curved
Weight 10 tons (9 tonnes)
Lived One million years ago

One steppe forward

The steppe mammoth *Mammuthus trogontherii* was far larger than any elephant today, and probably bigger than any other mammoth too. Its total nose–tail length was perhaps up to 45 ft (13.7 m), with a shoulder height of 16 ft (4.9 m). It may have weighed well over 14 tons (12 tonnes). Steppe mammoths lived on the vast grassy plains, or steppes, that were common across the north of Europe and Asia about half a million years ago.

SHARK
VERSUS
WHALE

Two supreme sea monsters—
Megalodon and *Livyatan*—ruled
the oceans 12 mya. These deep-water
devourers were among the most savage
creatures to ever swim the seas. But
what would have happened if these two
giants ever came head-to-head?

MEGALODON

Scientific name *Carcharodon megalodon*
Named 1843
Meaning "Ragged-toothed big-tooth"
Weight 50 tons (45 tonnes)
Length 52 ft (16 m)
Jaw width 11 ft (3.4 m)
Tooth length 6.3 in (16 cm)
Estimated maximum speed 35 mph (56 km/h)
Maneuverability Medium

Two mega predators

The middle Miocene Epoch saw both
Megalodon and *Livyatan* patroling the oceans—
this is when their eras overlapped. *Megalodon*,
the monster shark, was well established as a
top ocean predator, and would survive
another 10 million years. Fossils of the
enormous whale, *Livyatan*, are much
rarer, with only one main find so
far, in Peru, South America.

In the hot-blooded corner...

Contestant *Livyatan* was almost as massive as
the largest ocean predator on planet Earth
today—the sperm whale, which can reach 65 tons
(59 tonnes). Back in the Miocene era, *Livyatan*
was indeed the biggest ocean hunter—apart from
its deadly rival, *Megalodon*. The mighty
prehistoric whale was named Melville's sperm
whale after Herman Melville, author of an
exciting adventure story written in 1851 about
a sperm whale named Moby Dick.

STRENGTHS AND WEAKNESSES

Livyatan had size and bulk on its side.
Like all whales, it was warm-blooded
and breathed air, meaning it could
speed through cold seas faster than
Megalodon, but it was also at risk of
drowning if held under or disabled
beneath the surface. Its adaptable
mammalian intelligence might help
to outwit its opponent.

STRENGTHS AND WEAKNESSES

Megalodon's teeth were incredibly sharp, and its bite power was among the greatest of any animal. It was fast in warm seas, and its senses were highly tuned. But cold temperatures would slow it down, and its relatively unintelligent brain might not have been capable of working out what to do in a tactical battle.

In the cold-blooded corner...

Cruising the oceans from about 25 to 1.5 mya, *Megalodon* was a giant version of today's great white shark. This means we can guess how it lived and hunted based on what we know about its modern, small cousin. Like *Livyatan*, *Megalodon* would have attacked almost any sea life—fish, squid, smaller whales, dolphins, seals, sea lions, sea turtles, sea cows, sea birds—the list goes on. Its kind lasted over 20 million years, making it one of the most successful mega-predators in Earth's history.

LIVYATAN

Scientific name *Livyatan melvillei*
Named 2010
Meaning "Melville's leviathan"
Weight 55 tons (49 tonnes)
Length 51 ft (15.5 m)
Jaw length 9 ft (2.7 m)
Tooth length 14 in (35 cm)
Estimated maximum speed 25 mph (40 km/h)
Maneuverability Medium-poor

Battle breakdown

If these beasts had ever fought, *Megalodon* might have used its sharp teeth to attack rapidly, before retreating to wait for the whale to weaken. *Megalodon* might have attempted a full-frontal charge, hoping to break or bite through its adversary's slim lower jaw, but *Livyatan* could have counterattacked with a tremendous whack from its huge tail flukes, then twisted around to use its giant teeth!

Ice Age
MEGAFAUNA

Ice Ages have happened all through Earth's prehistory. The most recent filled much of the last 100,000 years and covered many northern lands with ice and snow. All kinds of large mammals, known as Ice Age mega fauna, roamed these cold regions, and were highly adapted to the bone-chilling winds and thick snow.

Measured around the curve, woolly mammoth tusks reached almost 16 ft (4.9 m).

▶ The enormous short-faced bear died out approximately 11,500 years ago.

At 3.5 tons (3.1 tonnes) and measuring 12 ft (3.6 m) in length, the woolly rhino was exceeded in size only by mammoths and their elephantine kin during the Ice Age.

The woolly rhino had two nose horns—the curved one at the front was up to 3 ft (90 cm) in length.

Warm rhino

Long, thick fur was a fantastic asset to ice age mammals. The woolly rhino was one of the hairiest, with a dense coat up to 5 inches (12.7 cm) thick—as shown by deep-frozen specimens that have been melted out of Siberian ice. Our ancestors' cave paintings show early humans attacking these rhinos, possibly with spears and other weapons—one very probable cause of its demise by 10,000 years ago.

Coldest and biggest

Today's biggest bears—the polar and grizzly—live in cold environments. This fits in with a natural principle called Bergmann's rule—within an animal group, such as elephants or bears, bigger species are found in colder environments. Their larger bodies have a lower proportion of surface for their volume, so they lose heat less quickly. The short-faced bear fitted this rule too —it was 8 ft (2.4 m) long and over 1.1 tons (1 tonne) in weight.

With a thick neck, massive head, and huge paws and claws, the short-faced bear was well equipped to hunt.

Superstar reborn?

One of the best known ice age mammals is the woolly mammoth. It was covered in hairs up to 3 ft (90 cm) long to preserve body heat in subzero temperatures. The science of genetics is progressing so fast, some experts think this extinct animal, and others, could one day be brought back from the dead. We would need the complete DNA set of genes—which we might find preserved in sites where mammoths, and similar creatures, deep-froze in the ice of the far north.

About 10 years old and 10 ft (3 m) long, "Yuka" the mammoth was almost perfectly preserved around 40,000 years ago.

ICE AGE ANIMALS DIED OUT IN THE LAST 20,000 YEARS, AROUND THE TIME EARTH'S CLIMATE BECAME RAPIDLY WARMER.

Saber-toothed cats like Smilodon had a powerful, muscular build and stood 4 ft (1.2 m) tall at the shoulder.

The largest *Smilodon* species was *S. populator*, which survived until perhaps 10,000 years ago.

Swords for teeth

Big ice age prey like mammoths, giant deer, and giant bison were hunted by great predators. The saber-toothed cat, *Smilodon,* of the Americas just outsized the largest cat today, the Siberian tiger, with a head-body length of 7 ft (2.1 m). It weighed an exceedingly heavy 840 lb (381 kg). *Smilodon's* curving, swordlike saber teeth were much more impressive than any true tiger—at 12 in (30 cm) long, they were excellent hunting tools, used to slash victims' flesh.

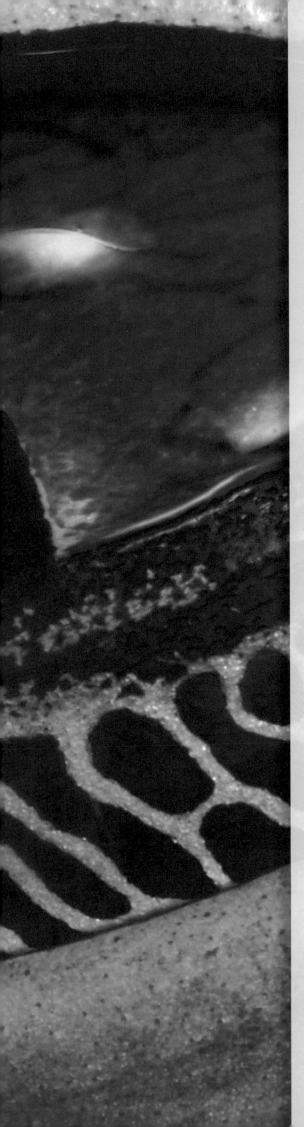

Awesome ANIMALS

In the wild, a fight for survival is taking place, and many creatures go to extremes to rise above the rest.

◀ The red-eyed tree frog has a thin membrane that partly covers its brightly colored eye. This allows the frog to see while remaining camouflaged.

Unusual
MOVES

All animals need to move to find food, seek shelter, escape enemies, and of course link up with breeding partners. Most creatures walk, run, fly, or swim, depending on their habitat, but some use unusual and unexpected ways of moving—such as flying with their feet!

Feet feats

From cheetahs and deer to ostriches and cockroaches, long, slim legs are a sure sign of speedy sprinters. There are many ways to get about on foot—kangaroos hop, grasshoppers leap, fleas jump, and some lizards and bugs even walk on water. However, few creatures are bipedal (move around regularly on two legs). A lizard may rear up briefly in fear, and an orangutan might amble along a branch, but only a select few—birds and humans—have the upright posture and delicate balance for bipedal walking.

△ The sifaka, a large Madagascan lemur, holds out its arms for balance while it moves using short, sideways hops.

The mudskipper uses its muscular armlike pectoral fins to haul its body across the tidal ooze. If in danger, this bizarre fish flips its whole body into the air to move to safety.

◁ Frogs usually use their webbed feet to provide a powerful push when swimming. However, the flying frog of Southeast Asia sails through the air using its webs like mini-parachutes to increase drag, slowing its descent.

Emergency aerobats

There's a massive difference between actual flying, like a bird, and a perilous leap into midair with just flaps of skin preventing a fatal plummet to the ground. "Flying" squirrels, lizards, frogs, and snakes don't actually fly, but glide. Their aerial ability is mainly used for emergencies. They create a broad surface, often by opening out flaps of skin, which encounters air resistance to slow their fall. A tilt or twist gives some control over direction, and a few bruises on landing are preferable to being gobbled up by a predator.

CLOCKED AT MORE THAN 65 MPH (105 KM/H), THE SAILFISH IS THE FASTEST SWIMMER IN THE WORLD.

▶ Using its partly webbed toes and fast strides, the basilisk lizard races on its hind legs across water—with no time to sink.

Water sports

Muscle-packed bodies and thrashing fins give fish speed—the fastest species, such as the sailfish, have stiff, narrow, crescent-shaped tails. However, fins are adaptable and can be used for out-of-water movement, too, such as in the goby and walking catfish. Bird wings are similar in shape to fins and some birds use them to thrust through water rather than air. Kingfishers and dippers can "swim" briefly, but penguins have given up air flight completely and only "fly" underwater.

▲ The kingfisher, using its wings as both rudders and underwater brakes, strikes with astonishing accuracy.

COOL Senses

All around are more light rays, sounds, and smells than humans could ever imagine. Animals of all kinds can tune into this abundance of sensations with their amazing supersenses. Often an animal is almost entirely dependent on just one dominant sense—block a bat's ears or an anteater's nostrils and they cannot survive.

▶ Giant anteaters sniff out their tiny quarry from more than 150 ft (45 m) away.

▶ The male cockchafer beetle's feathery antennae (feelers) detect scent particles, called pheromones, from females up to several miles away. These pheromone messages tell the male that the females are ready to mate.

Sniff, snort, snuffle

A polar bear can sniff out a seal carcass up to 4.5 mi (7 km) away, while a human would need to be within 300 ft (90 m) to detect even a trace of this rotting stench. Bears, wolves, and dogs far exceed a human's capacity because they have more than 200 million microscopic smell cells in their noses, compared to a human's five million. The sense of smell is not just for finding food. Without it, elephants would die of thirst, lions would not be able to mark their territory, and many moths and beetles could never detect scents released by potential mates that tell them they are ready to breed.

RHINO Sight estimated at five times poorer than a human's—it cannot distinguish between another rhino and a jeep at 300 ft (90 m) away. However, its sense of smell is ten times better than a human's.

EAGLE Sight is at least ten times better than a human's—it can see a rabbit more than 2 mi (3 km) away.

BAT Hearing can pick up vibrations ten times faster than a human—so it can hear a tiny gnat's flapping wings.

MOTH Sense of smell is more than 10,000 times more sensitive than a human's—it can scent nectar from a blossom that a human could not even see in daylight!

▲ A bat finds its way around using echolocation—it squeaks and then listens to the echoes to work out where objects in its path are. Large ears help a bat to gather these sounds. If a human's ears were relative in size to the long-eared bat's, they would be bigger than trashcan lids!

Hear, hear!

A noise that sounds quiet to a human might deafen an owl or a bat. They have far more microsensors in their ears, and they move their ears or head much more carefully to receive the maximum number of sound waves and pinpoint an object's position. Ears are not always on the head. Insects such as grasshoppers and crickets have them on their knees, and some fish "hear" with their swim bladders.

Seeing the invisible

Animal eyes can see infrared and ultraviolet light—both of which are outside the spectrum of light that is visible to humans. Insects in particular are highly tuned to these invisible wavelengths. To a bee, plain-looking petals are covered with ultraviolet lines that point to the sweet nectar inside. Some fish have an amazing sense of sight, too. Piranhas can see the warm, infrared glow of a mammal—then launch their mass attack.

▲ Finding and attacking prey is no problem for a jumping spider. They have two huge eyes to see objects in great detail and color. The remaining six eyes detect movement and create a large field of vision.

The GROSS Factor

Animals have some disgusting habits. To deter predators, they spray vomit or excrement, spit saliva, and even squirt blood from open vessels. When it comes to feeding, they certainly have no manners—tearing at flesh and creating a bloody mess. Some animals even tuck into excrement for a tasty snack.

THE HORNED LIZARD SQUIRTS A BLOODY FLUID FROM ITS EYES—MORE THAN 5 FT (1.5 M)—AT A THREAT.

Disgusting defense

Vomit, slime, urine, droppings, spit, and pus can sting, cause infection, and create an off-putting stench. Some animals capitalize on this by using their bodily fluids to make enemies recoil and retreat. The innocent-looking sea cucumber throws up its super-sticky guts over an attacker, while several kinds of seabird projectile vomit more than 3 ft (1 m) at an enemy.

▼ The world's largest lizards have big appetites. Komodo dragons feast on a rotting dolphin carcass, enjoying the fatty blubber and the guts filled with semidigested fish. Male komodos can reach lengths of 10 ft (3 m).

Feeding frenzy

Even before a huge pile of food becomes available, predators and scavengers wait in the wings. A dying whale is tracked by sharks, orcas, and seabirds, while a sick elephant lures hyenas, jackals, and vultures. As soon as one plucks up the courage to move in for a mouthful, the rest rush to grab what they can. The feeding frenzy that follows is rough, gory, and urgent as they push and scrap to get the best share before it's all gone.

Messy breeders

Animal babies can be born in the most disgusting conditions. Some parasitic wasp grubs hatch in the guts of a caterpillar, and proceed to eat the host alive. Dung beetle grubs emerge from their eggs into balls of excrement. Surinam toad tadpoles develop inside their mother's back, under her skin. Other frogs whip up a foam using a cocktail of their saliva, skin slime, sperm fluid, and excrement, and lay their eggs here.

▼ A group of male gray foam-nest tree frogs cluster around one female and whip their bodily fluids into a froth, in which she deposits her spawn.

Nasty nourishment

Dung, droppings, and excrement might look and smell horrible. However, the digestion of most animals is not very efficient, so feces often still contain plenty of nutrients. Dung eaters usually like to get it while it's fresh, before molds, germs, and flies arrive to contaminate the rotting mass.

▲ This turkey vulture quickly devours fishy feces from a fur seal.

49

Wicked
ASSASSINS

Natural born killers are feared for their deadly weapons. These fearsome animals mercilessly slay their prey with lethal teeth, claws, and fangs, devouring flesh, bones, and blood with ease—no morsel is spared.

Wolfie the Wolffish

Last seen in the waters of the Atlantic Ocean, the wolffish is 5 ft (1.5 m) long and can be recognized by its vast number of teeth. It has about 100 of them—fanglike at the front, broad for crushing at the back, and continuing into its throat. Its typical victims are shellfish, starfish, crabs, and urchins, which the wolffish crushes to death with great power.

WANTED

Terminator
the Alligator

This 15-ft- (4.6-m-) long 'gator is wanted for drowning prey by dragging it underwater. Victims include turtles, snakes, waterbirds, and mammals up to the size of deer. Beware—the alligator is armed and dangerous, with 50 cone-shaped teeth and amazingly strong jaw muscles. Do not approach.

WANTED
REWARD $2,000

JAW
THE GRIZZLY BEAR

Towering up to 10 (3 m) tall, the grizzly a formidable hunte Its weapons includ powerful teeth and jaws plate-sized paws, and curved claws. These features, combined with enormous weight, power, and stamina, mean that nothing is safe. The grizzly will attack anything up to the size of moose and never lets go.

FANG THE GABOON VIPER

The Gaboon viper is a massive 6 ft (2 m) long. Mice, rats, birds, and similar small creatures have been found dead, marked with puncture wounds. This cold-blooded killer strikes at lightning speed, using its long, foldout front fangs to stab the victim's flesh and inject deadly venom. It then waits for the victim to die of shock as the heart stops beating (cardiac arrest).

WANTED
DEAD OR ALIVE

Lurking in the shadows of the deep, the 11-ft- (3.5-m-) long sand tiger shark charges suddenly, taking its victim by surprise. Fish, squid, shellfish, and crabs have all suffered from this menace's slashing bite.

SMILER THE SAND TIGER SHARK

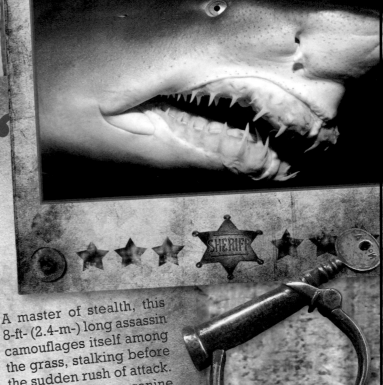

SHERIFF

MOST WANTED

A master of stealth, this 8-ft- (2.4-m-) long assassin camouflages itself among the grass, stalking before the sudden rush of attack. Armed with huge canine teeth and slicing back teeth, victims are killed with a throat-crushing bite, before the lion tears its flesh apart using sharp, curved claws. An experienced killer, no "hit" is too big or small for this ferocious feline. Its kill list includes gazelles and antelope, as well as rats and beetles.

BABOONS OFTEN KILL OTHER BABOONS TO BECOME THE BOSS OF THE TROOP.

CLAWS THE LION

Deadly
DEFENSE

The forest is nearly dark and almost quiet. A creature sneaks up on the juicy meal it has been tracking. It steadies itself, preparing to pounce... WOAH! Suddenly two huge eyes appear, glaring in the gloom. A big cat? A snake? An owl? No, they're eyespots (false eyes)—one of many animal self-defense tactics.

Terrible taste

Having horrible-tasting or poisonous flesh deters predators and works as a great group defense strategy. After biting one foul-tasting animal, a hunter learns to recognize its warning signs, such as colors and patterns, and stays away from all similar-looking prey.

◀ The African foam grasshopper shows its nasty taste by blowing noxious bubbles from tiny breathing holes, called spiracles, along its body.

Animal armor

Some creatures lack speed to escape enemies, or foul-tasting defenses to deter them. Instead they use simple physical protection. Tough-shelled animals include crabs, clams, and snails, as well as armadillos and pangolins. They simply shut up tight and wait for the danger to pass.

▶ The three-banded armadillo has bony plates within its skin, covered by outer scales of horny keratin. Its armor is so flexible that it can curl into a tight ball that will completely defeat predators.

◀ A rear view of the peacock katydid (a type of grasshopper) shows how its suddenly raised wings display enormous eyespots to startle a potential attacker.

Guns blazing

Camouflage is a great defense tactic. An animal that matches the background color of its habitat can just sit still and hope to go unnoticed. But what if it's spotted? The next tactic is to make a grand show of defense—rear up, look big, reveal your weapons, make a noise, wave and shake, and generally try to look as frightening and inedible as possible.

▶ If its disguise is rumbled, the dead-leaf mantis raises its body and extends its wings and fearsome, spiked, jackknife forelegs to appear super-fierce.

Young and Old

Why do elephants live longer than flies? These creatures are at two ends of a whole spectrum of life strategies. One is to develop slowly, and take great care of just a few young. The other is to live fast and die young, mating frequently and producing lots of offspring but providing no parental care.

4 MONTHS

Congratulations!

Labord's chameleon

Shortest-lived of any four-legged vertebrate, this lizard's life cycle is perfectly adapted to Madagascar's seasonal changes. It lives for a single year, spending eight months in an egg and just four months in its adult form.

1 DAY!

Have a Great Day!

happy birthday!

1 TODAY!

Brine shrimp

Old shrimps lay tough-cased eggs before their salt lake dries up for summer. When it starts to rain in fall, the eggs hatch, and the next generation begins to feed.

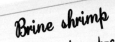

I AM 3 WEEKS OLD

Bee Happy!

Mayfly

The mayfly spends a year or two as an underwater nymph. Then it emerges, molts to reveal its wonderful wings, mates in midair, and dies—all within 24 hours.

Worker honeybee

Day after day of nonstop toil means the worker honeybee's body suffers immense wear and tear. The egg-laying queen might make it to five years old.

50!

Macaw
Several parrot species may reach the half-century mark. Intelligence—along with their powerful beaks and claws—help these birds to survive.

BIRTHDAY GREETINGS!

70 Today

Elephant
Size and power provide protection against lions and other foes, and family ties mean younger and more vulnerable members of the herd are well-guarded by the females of the group.

175

giant birthday!

Giant tortoise
Life in the slow lane, with a reptile's unhurried body chemistry, plentiful food, few natural predators, and a thick, protective shell, is a great recipe for reaching a great age.

220
TODAY
220
HAPPY BIRTHDAY

Koi carp
These precious and pampered ornamental fish are popular pets because they reach a great age, in addition to their beautiful coloration.

Quahog clam
This shellfish holds the record for the longest life (and perhaps the most boring—it spends all of its many days lying on the dark seabed).

400
TODAY!

Dinner TIME

In the wild, animals rarely know where their next meal is coming from, so any snack is greedily gobbled up. If a glut of food appears, some species will eat until they are almost bursting—the opportunity to devour their fill may not come again.

▶ The Bryde's whale spends all day filtering tiny creatures such as krill and small fish from the water. Its daily diet can weigh 3 tons—equivalent to the amount of food eaten by a human over a period of seven or eight years.

▼ This African bullfrog has no teeth and cannot tear up or chew its mouse victim. Instead, frogs and toads feed by stretching their head-wide mouths and gulping prey whole.

Down in one

The bodies of many creatures are adapted for eating huge amounts in a single feeding session. Features range from a stretchy stomach to a dislocating jaw. With scavengers and enemies lurking everywhere, fast food is best—rapid gulps or the all-in-one swallow. After gorging their fill, these gluttons can hide away from danger while they digest.

Leave it in the larder

Some animals store excess food for later, to avoid waste and prepare for periods when food is scarce. Squirrels bury nuts, crocodiles wedge gazelles beneath underwater rocks, and tigers scrape leaves and soil over deer carcasses. These clever methods mean these creatures are less likely to die of starvation when times are hard.

▶ The leopard can haul a kill three times its own weight up into a tree, away from scavengers such as jackals.

▼ These white-backed vultures rush to peck the juiciest morsels from a dead giraffe, before pack of hyenas arrive on the scene.

Scavenger hunt

Old meat is still a valuable source of nourishment, so a large carcass attracts a multitude of scavengers. The first (airborne vultures) and the fiercest (hyena clans) get the richest pickings. Lesser scavengers such as jackals soon follow.

After a lightning, twist-and-turn chase, the leopard seal strikes with its viciously sharp canine teeth. The seal moves in as the penguin weakens, and chomps away at the fatty blubber and tasty flesh.

Bite to kill

Any predator must make careful decisions about which prey to tackle, and how. If an animal has just eaten, it may feel full and sluggish, and this might put it off tackling another large victim. A predator will also assess the fitness of potential prey—is it strong and healthy, or (preferably) too young, old, or sick, for its defenses to prove a problem? The attack itself must be swift and decisive, since in the wild even a slight injury makes a hunter far less capable.

The Perfect Animal?

Every species is superbly adapted to its habitat and way of life. But some creatures' features are super-adapted, compared to other, similar animals. If we could bring together all these extreme adaptations into one combi-creature, surely it would instantly be crowned king of the animal kingdom?

Ringtailed lemur's TAIL

Not only an excellent balance aid, the lemur's tail is used to convey signals about mood and intention. The male sprays a nasty scent on its own tail and waves it at opponents to mark its territory. The tail also indicates an individual's rank within the group, and attracts a mate.

Cheetah's BODY

Slim and streamlined, the fastest land animal's body is lithe yet muscular and flexible, and ideal for out-sprinting prey.

Gerenuk's HIND LEGS

Slim and strong, this antelope rears up on its hind legs to reach juicy leaves in tall trees—food that few other animals can reach.

Elephant's EARS
Not only brilliant for catching faint sounds, the world's biggest ears can flap both to lose internal heat and to fan cooling air over the body.

Tarsier's EYES
The tarsier hunts by grabbing passing moths and bats, so its massive eyes have a fabulous ability to follow fast motion, as well as superb vision even on the darkest nights.

Tiger's MOUTH
Huge, sharp teeth and one of the biggest, strongest bites of any land animal ensures that any victim is fatally wounded in an instant.

Proboscis monkey's NOSE
Long and drooping, this remarkable nose amplifies hoots and calls, and also offers a superior sense of smell compared to other monkey species.

Giraffe's NECK
As well as reaching far higher food than any other ground-bound animal, a giraffe's excellent vantage point gives it an all-round aerial view—so it can spot approaching predators from a long way off.

Kangaroo's LEGS
The kangaroo's hind legs offer an energy-efficient, bouncing gait, with the added extra of huge leaps 26 ft (8 m) long and 13 ft (4 m) high.

The natural world is both nice and nasty, when animals of two different species live together in a symbiotic relationship. Here, both partners help each other in some way for mutual benefit.

As the clownfish swims around the anemone, water circulation increases, which helps the anemone to breathe.

Best of friends

Sea anemones and clownfish work together in harmony. Although anemones feed by paralyzing small fish with their stinging tentacles, the clownfish's slimy coating resists the venom. The anemone recognizes this and rarely attempts to attack. In return for this safe haven, the clownfish eats debris and pests among the tentacles to keep the anemone clean. The anemone also scares off animals that may prey on clownfish, while the clownfish lures in other fish to be eaten by the anemone.

► Ants crowd around the aphids and "milk" them so they secrete sweet, sugar-rich honeydew.

Buddies vs

Baddies

Sometimes partnerships are horribly one-sided. One benefits, while the other gets hurt—the parasite-host situation. But being a parasite is a balancing act. If you are too successful, all your hosts die out and you have nowhere to live and nothing to eat.

Eaten alive

Some of the nastiest parasites are small wasps that lay their eggs in living caterpillars and other larvae. The wasp stings and paralyzes the caterpillar, then deposits its eggs inside the host's body. The wasp grubs hatch and proceed to eat the helpless host bit by bit.

▼ This tomato hornworm caterpillar is covered with parasitic wasp eggs. Its death will be slow as the hatched grubs chomp away until all that's left is an empty skin.

Protection for food

Aphids (greenfly and blackfly) are tiny, soft, and defenseless—except when they are in the care of an ant colony. While the aphids feed on plant sap with their sucking mouthparts, ants from a nearby nest patrol the region and keep away aphid enemies, such as ladybugs. In return for their protection, the ants feed on a sugary liquid, called honeydew, produced by the aphids.

▼ This impala is being "cleaned" by red-billed oxpeckers. Although they get rid of pests, oxpeckers may also peck at their host's skin, keeping wounds open—making this bird both a helper and a parasite.

A quick cleanup

The oxpecker doesn't only peck oxen—it may debug antelope, gazelles, giraffes, zebras, rhinos... as well as many more. The bird feeds on pests, such as lice, fleas, and ticks, especially in hard-to-reach places, as well as blood from any open wounds.

▶ This common cuckoo fledgling dwarfs its eager dunnock foster parent. The dunnock's instinct to feed its young is so strong, it fails to recognize that this giant youngster is an imposter.

Crafty cuckoo

A brood parasite takes advantage of other animals at breeding time, using them to raise its own offspring. The female cuckoo lays her egg in another bird's nest. The chick hatches, pushes out the other eggs, and demands food from its new parents. Other brood parasites include cowbirds, whydahs, and honeyguides.

SHOWTIME
Spectacular!

Most creatures spend their time keeping a low profile, trying to stay unnoticed by predators. But there are times when an animal needs to make itself known, showing off any special features, either to attract a mate or to discourage a rival or enemy from approaching.

FLICKER, FLASH
The female **glowworm** is actually a wingless beetle and glows to attract a winged male for mating.

DRESS UP
A male **ruff** erects his beautiful soft collar of pale feathers as he struts and calls when breeding.

KICK, PUNCH
A female **hare** plays hard to get as she "boxes" with a male to test his health, speed, reactions, and vigor.

BLOW UP
A male **greater frigate** stretches his gular (throat) pouch to show his potential as a mating partner.

Courting couples

Animal courtship is not just a quick flirt for fun—it's a serious test. Each partner checks the other is the correct species, strong and healthy, and will pass on good genes to any offspring.

FAN OUT
A **peacock** fans out his shimmering, green tail to impress a peahen. The brighter the colors, the more attractive his tail appears.

FEED ME
A **European bee-eater** pair give each other food morsels as they flutter like butterflies when courting.

PUFF OUT
The male **hooded seal** impresses potential partners by inflating a balloon of skin out of its nose.

FLAG UP
A courting male **anole lizard** flicks out his colorful throat fan, or dewlap, to attract a mate.

Bright SPARKS

Q: What do chimps, dolphins, octopuses, elephants, parrots, dogs, and monkeys have in common?

A: They are some of the animal world's smartest cookies. Their range of talents—including tool use, problem solving, and teamwork—make them top of the class.

Using tools

Many animals have developed incredible techniques to obtain food otherwise unattainable for them. The Egyptian vulture uses a stone as a hammer to crack a tough egg, while the woodpecker finch extracts grubs from tree holes with a cactus spine. The master is the chimp—it not only uses tools, but also modifies them. For example, it chews the end of its termite "fishing stick" to make it sleeker and easier to poke into the mound.

The Egyptian vulture drops a stone onto an ostrich egg to break it open and feed on the nutritious contents.

Chimps have developed a clever way to collect termites. They poke a stem into a termite nest, then simply withdraw it and lick off the termites.

This veined octopus carries a discarded cockle shell for shelter.

Problem solving

Problem: if you are soft-bodied, how do you guard against hungry enemies? Solution: borrow someone else's protection. The hermit crab uses this technique and will try on several old whelk shells for size to find the best fit. Small fish and octopuses also take advantage of empty seashells as temporary shelters.

Dolphins "talk" using clicks and squeaks as they corral sardines into a baitball, where they can be picked off easily.

SPECIAL STORAGE

The acorn woodpecker slots acorns and other nuts into purpose-pecked bark cracks, adding more holes each year.

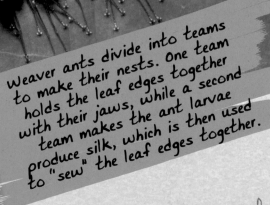

Weaver ants divide into teams to make their nests. one team holds the leaf edges together with their jaws, while a second team makes the ant larvae produce silk, which is then used to "sew" the leaf edges together.

Dream team

Each member of an animal team knows its place and its purpose within the group. Ants are preprogrammed to only follow a few simple instincts, so rarely adapt to new situations. With a decreasing fish population in the oceans, dolphins, however, have developed new methods of finding food—such as chasing trawler nets laden with fish, to feed on any escapees.

abcdef 2×2=4

Strength in NUMBERS

Living and working together in a group can offer some species many advantages. With more animals, there is a greater number of resources—more eyes on the lookout, more defensive weapons to protect the young, and more teeth and claws to attack prey.

Mighty migration

Animals go on annual or seasonal journeys, called migrations, usually due to changes in climate or a seasonal lack of food. Every year, at the start of the wet season (October–November), Christmas Island red crabs move across the shore like an unstoppable red tide, marching into the sea to lay eggs in their millions.

Body building

An inconvenient gap in the path is no problem for a swarming ant colony, especially when they are army ants on the march. The ants simply build a bridge from their own bodies. Neighboring ants lock legs as more climb over them to lengthen the interlinked chains. The bridging ants may stay like this for hours, and even die, as their fellow workers surge over and resume the search

Savage swarms

Locusts require a few months of good conditions to breed and build up their numbers. Gradually, they form an enormous gathering, capable of completely consuming vegetation across an entire region. Continuously in search of fresh greenery, swarms containing hundreds of millions of locusts can quickly ravage farm crops.

Hound dogs

African wild dogs can take down large prey, up to 20 times their own size—using teamwork. The lead dog picks out a young, old, or sick quarry such as a wildebeest. With dogged determination the pack hounds the desperate victim for many miles, until it is so weak from exhaustion that they can move in for the kill.

ANY HINT OF BLOOD IN THE WATER SENDS A GROUP OF RED-BELLIED PIRANHAS INTO A FEEDING FRENZY. WITH DOZENS OF SETS OF RAZOR-SHARP SLASHING TEETH, THEIR FEROCIOUS ATTACK IS IMMEDIATE AND OFTEN FATAL.

Strange Babies

Many animal parents have strong caring instincts, and will even risk their lives to save their babies. Some creatures go to extremes to give their offspring the best chance of survival. The young of some species are born while still at an early stage of development, when they are vulnerable and require constant care. They also look nothing like their parents—in fact, some animal babies look very odd indeed.

▼ A female giant panda gives birth to a single cub, which may stay with her for two years or more. Once a cub is weaned (after the first year), the mother may leave it for days at a time, while she forages for food.

Mini me or metamorphosis?

Some animal offspring, such as seal pups and tiger cubs, are unmistakable mini versions of their parents. Others, such as tadpoles and caterpillars, change dramatically from birth to adulthood. These drastic changes in shape, called metamorphoses, allow the youngsters to live in different environments and eat different foods from the parents, to avoid competing against each other.

Pink and hairless

Many newborn mammals and birds are born when they are still pink and hairless. Their eyes and ears are closed, and they can only feed and sleep. The mother can leave them to find food for herself—once the youngsters are hidden in a nest or a burrow. Her offspring are entirely dependent on her for protection and food.

◀▲ Most caterpillars hatch from eggs a few days after they are laid. They consume vast amounts of leaves before pupating inside a chrysalis and emerging in their adult form to feed on flower nectar.

▼ Seal cubs look just like their parents, except they are born with white fur. They feed on their mother's rich milk and grow faster than any other mammal of their size.

► A newborn kangaroo doesn't have proper arms or legs. Yet straight away it has to climb from the birth opening and through its mother's fur to her pouch. Then it attaches to a teat, and stays there for six months until ready to leave the pouch.

Born at an early age

Marsupial mammals such as kangaroos, koalas, wombats, and possums are born at a very early stage of development. Many do not even have recognizable eyes or ears, and their limbs are just flaps or "buds" on the featureless body. These newborns do little except wriggle to the mother's pouch, or marsupium, latch onto a teat with their barely formed mouth, and feed on her milk. Within the protection of the pouch, they continue the stages of development that other mammals go through while still in the womb.

► The Virginia opossum may have more tiny pink babies (below) than she has teats. Some die so that the survivors can grow big enough for a ride (above).

Brilliant Builders

Animals create some amazing structures, whether building alone or in groups. Everything they build is for a purpose—a nest to protect their young, a bridge to get from one place to another, or a trap to capture prey. Building methods can vary, depending on what materials are available in a particular habitat.

Supersize it

Some creatures make massive constructions compared to their size. Termites are insects that are only the size of peas, yet their mounds can tower more than 32 ft (10 m) high—that's equivalent to a skyscraper more than 1.5 mi (2.5 km) tall. Other outsizers dig down deep. A network of tunnels built by prairie dogs in Texas, U.S., covered 23,000 sq mi (60,000 sq km) and housed 400 million of these rodents— 20 times more people than in the largest cities.

Actual-size termite

Adult human

20-ft termite mound

◀ Much of the termite mound above the ground is hollow chimneys, made of sun-baked earth. They provide air-conditioning to the main nest below ground level.

◀ The masked weaver tears leaves and stems into strips and delicately intertwines them to create its ball- or flask-shaped nest.

Perfect homemakers

Animals often build nests or burrows to live in for just a short time, usually to raise their young. Most of their behavior is instinctive, but skills and techniques improve greatly with practice. Nests can be made out of a wide range of natural materials, such as grass and mud, as well as materials from other animals, such as feathers and fur.

▶ The breeding nest of the harvest mouse is hardly larger than a tennis ball. It is built in between stems, high above the ground, to protect the young from danger.

◀▼ A beaver lodge can reach up to 65 ft (20 m) wide and 16 ft (5 m) high.

My home is my castle

The beaver's house, or lodge, is a solid construction of branches, rocks, twigs, and mud. Each generation of beavers carefully fells trees, gnaws off boughs, and adds reinforcements to make an amazing fortress that even hungry wolves and bears cannot break into.

Super STRENGTH

Heavyweight

Elephants can lift logs and other objects weighing up to one ton with their trunks—but the elephant has a great body weight, too, at 5 tons. So a fairer measure of strength is to compare weight moved against body weight—for an elephant, this is just 1/5.

Elephants are the strongest of all land animals, but that's mainly due to their great size.

AN ELEPHANT CAN LIFT ONE FIFTH OF ITS OWN BODY WEIGHT.

A WEASEL CAN LIFT 30 TIMES MORE THAN ITS OWN BODY WEIGHT.

Human weightlifters can hoist more than three times their body weight, but that's puny compared to some insects. We are weaklings in other ways too, like our jumping ability, pulling power, or bite strength. But we are champions in one way— as athletic all-rounders.

Weasels are the world's smallest carnivores, with some individuals weighing little more than one ounce (30 g). They must eat at least one third of their own body weight every day to survive, and can bring down rabbits weighing 35 oz (one kilogram) or more.

A DUNG BEETLE CAN PULL MORE THAN 1,000 TIMES ITS OWN BODY WEIGHT.

Dung beetles can roll balls of fresh dung up to 30 times more than their own body weight.

ANTS CAN LIFT UP TO 50 TIMES MORE THAN THEIR OWN BODY WEIGHT AND CAN CARRY THE LOAD OVER A DISTANCE OF MANY FEET.

Rolling home

Dung beetles roll excrement—from animals including rhinos, wolves, antelopes, elephants, and cats—into balls. While the dung is still moist, the beetles roll the balls to a suitable place, lay eggs inside them, and bury them. The grubs then feed on the dung when they hatch.

Bite size

Bite power depends on whether the biter is angry or relaxed, and whether it uses all its teeth and jaws. Lions, hyenas, sharks, and crocodiles are all super-crunchers, able to crush the bones of prey with ease. However, the extinct dinosaur *T rex* probably had the strongest bite of any animal that has ever lived.

A SHARK CAN BITE 60 TIMES HARDER THAN A HUMAN.

▶ Great white sharks have a strong bite, but the real damage comes from its razor-sharp teeth that can easily saw through flesh and bone.

Can You See Me?

O ne of the oldest tricks in the animal world is for your body shape, color, pattern, or texture to mimic your surroundings. Camouflage is all about visual trickery and blending in, whether it's to stay unnoticed by enemies or lurk unseen near prey.

A broken-off tree stump merits no second look. Just as well for the great potoo, a night-hunting bird that must stay completely still by day.

Acting the part

Camouflage depends not only on colors, patterns, and shapes, but on movements, too. It's no good merging perfectly into the surroundings, if a sudden movement gives the game away. To be successful, camouflaged creatures must move with extreme care. If the leaf it is resting on blows in the wind, the animal must hang on and sway with it, or risk discovery.

The imperial moth is highly camouflaged on the forest floor, and must rustle and flip with the real leaf litter.

To remain concealed, the leaf-tail gecko must mimic the random motion of a dead leaf—whether remaining motionless or moving with the breeze.

Peering faces

Some predators are not so much well camouflaged as well hidden. Forest frogs, desert toads, and soil-dwelling spiders burrow into the ground, leaving only their eyes and ears exposed to detect passing prey. They must stay like this for hours, until their victim relaxes and strays within reach of their lightning strike.

The Chacoan horned frog almost buries itself in soil, waiting for a beetle or grub to pass by.

A SHARK'S COLORING HELPS IT TO SNEAK UP ON PREY—ITS DARK BACK BLENDS WITH THE SEABED, WHILE ITS PALE BELLY MATCHES THE LIGHTER WATER ABOVE. THIS IS KNOWN AS "COUNTERSHADING."

The nose and eyes of the sidewinding adder match the grains of desert sand around it, hiding it almost completely from view as it waits patiently for its next victim.

Lurking danger

The bigger you are, the more difficult it is to hide from your prey. Big cats have some of the best camouflage colors and patterns, with each species well adapted to its main habitat. Lions are tawny to match the African savanna's dry grasses and dusty soils. Tiger stripes blend in with undergrowth and shrubs, and are particularly effective in the half-light when they are usually out hunting. Leopards and jaguars tend to stay among trees, and their spots mimic the dappled shadows cast by the twigs and leaves above.

A lion peers through the African grassland, perfectly color-matched to its surroundings, on the lookout for food—and danger.

The Big Lineup

Monster creatures are thriving all over the planet. A big animal can usually see off predators easily, and is likely to be strong and able to reach food that others can't. On the downside, these giants have to find and eat lots of food to get the energy they need to survive.

BLUE WHALE
Largest animal ever known

105 FT (32 M) Length of its body

198 TONS Weight of its body

3.5 TONS Weight of food it eats in one day

25 FT (7.6 M) Width of its tail

6 TONS Weight of its tongue

30 MPH (48 KM/H) Top swimming speed

1,300 LB (600 KG) Weight of its heart

TALLEST BIRD
Not only is the **OSTRICH** the tallest and heaviest bird, it is also the fastest, reaching a speed of 60 mph (96 km/h). This gigantic bird lays the largest eggs in the world, at 3 lb (1.4 kg) in weight.

LARGEST APE
The large size of the male **GORILLA** allows it to defend its group from attack with intimidating displays involving charging, roaring, and chest beating.

LARGEST MARSUPIAL
Male **RED KANGAROOS** are built for power, with strong tails and sharp claws. When trying to win a female, males can fight or "box" each other, delivering powerful kicks with their muscular hind legs.

OSTRICH
HEIGHT: UP TO 8.8 FT (2.7 M)
WEIGHT: UP TO 310 LB (140 KG)

KODIAK BROWN BEAR
HEIGHT: 7.8 FT (2.4 M)
WEIGHT: UP TO 1,200 LB (545 KG)

RED KANGAROO
HEIGHT: 5.2 FT (1.6 M)
WEIGHT: UP TO 200 LB (90 KG)

GORILLA
HEIGHT: 6 FT (1.8 M)
WEIGHT: UP TO 440 LB (220 KG)

SIBERIAN TIGER
LENGTH: 11 FT (3.3 M) HEAD TO TAIL TIP
WEIGHT: UP TO 660 LB (300 KG)

LARGEST LAND CARNIVORE
The **KODIAK BROWN BEAR** uses its large size to intimidate other large predators. Although battles are rare, its massive strength and size usually results in it winning any violent conflicts.

LARGEST CAT
A powerful, heavily muscled predator, the **SIBERIAN TIGER** uses stalk-and-ambush tactics to bring down large prey, such as deer, single-handedly.

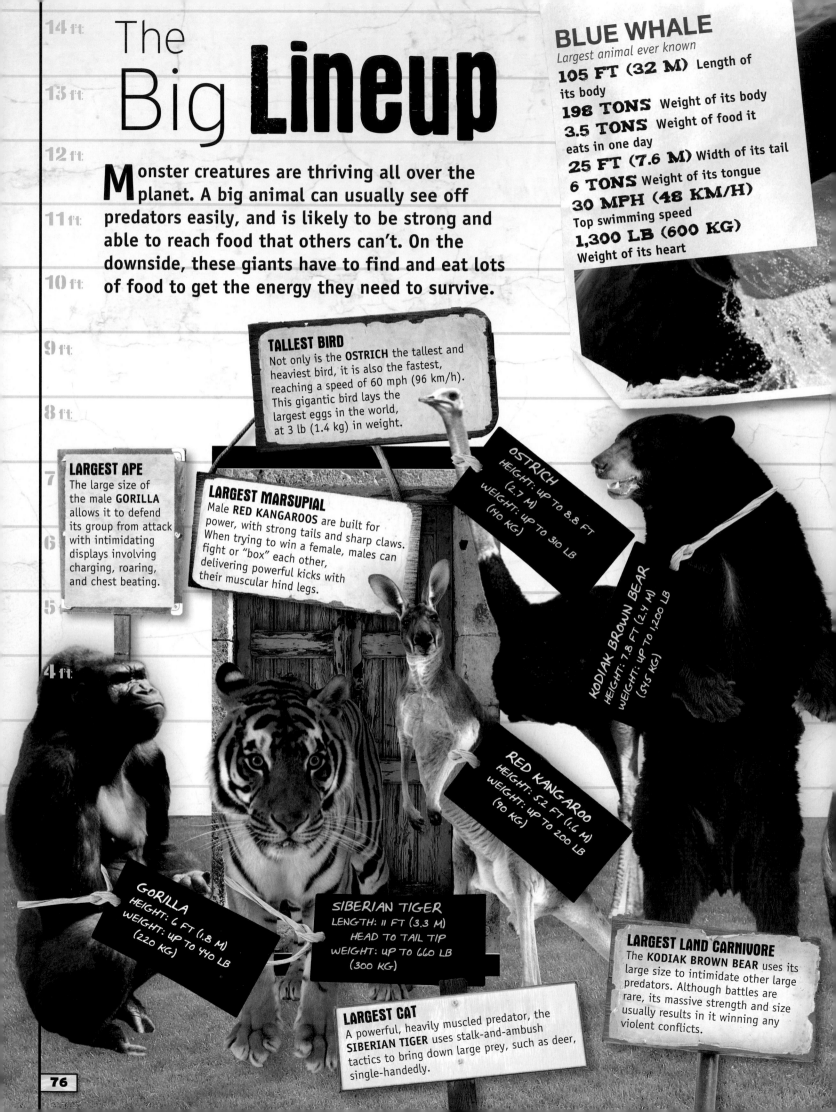

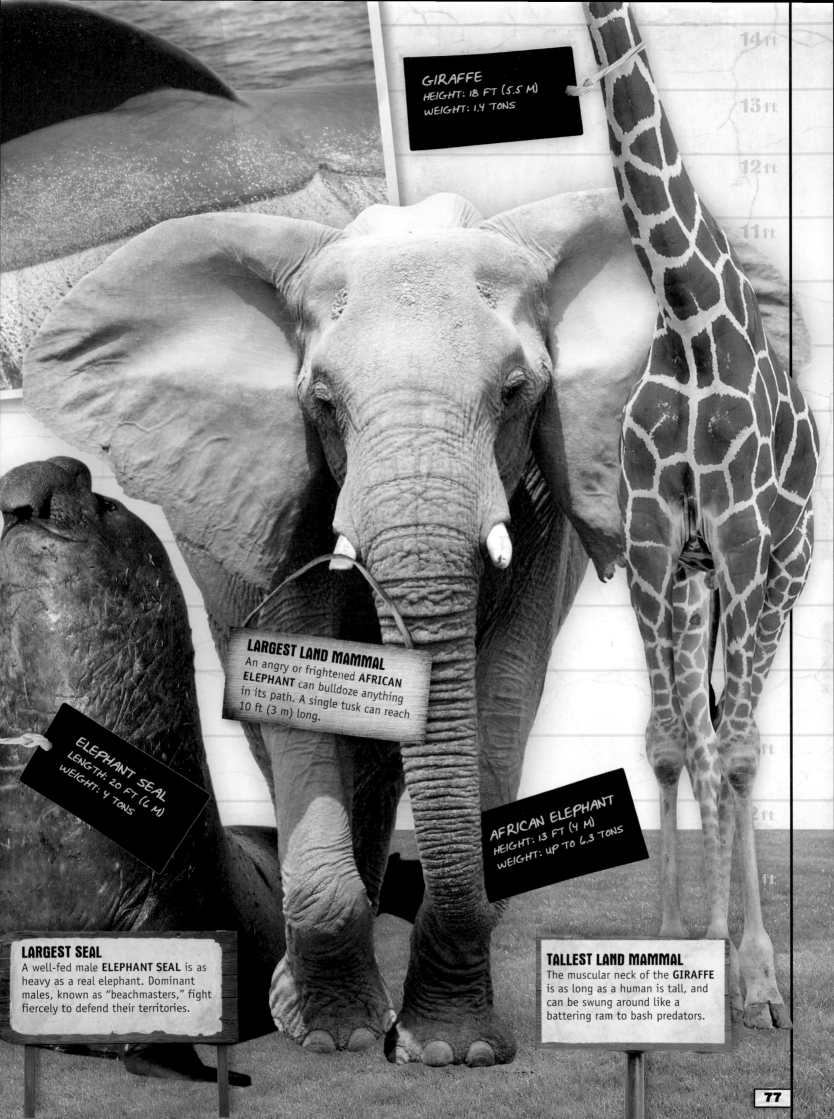

GIRAFFE
HEIGHT: 18 FT (5.5 M)
WEIGHT: 1.4 TONS

LARGEST LAND MAMMAL
An angry or frightened **AFRICAN ELEPHANT** can bulldoze anything in its path. A single tusk can reach 10 ft (3 m) long.

ELEPHANT SEAL
LENGTH: 20 FT (6 M)
WEIGHT: 4 TONS

AFRICAN ELEPHANT
HEIGHT: 13 FT (4 M)
WEIGHT: UP TO 6.3 TONS

LARGEST SEAL
A well-fed male **ELEPHANT SEAL** is as heavy as a real elephant. Dominant males, known as "beachmasters," fight fiercely to defend their territories.

TALLEST LAND MAMMAL
The muscular neck of the **GIRAFFE** is as long as a human is tall, and can be swung around like a battering ram to bash predators.

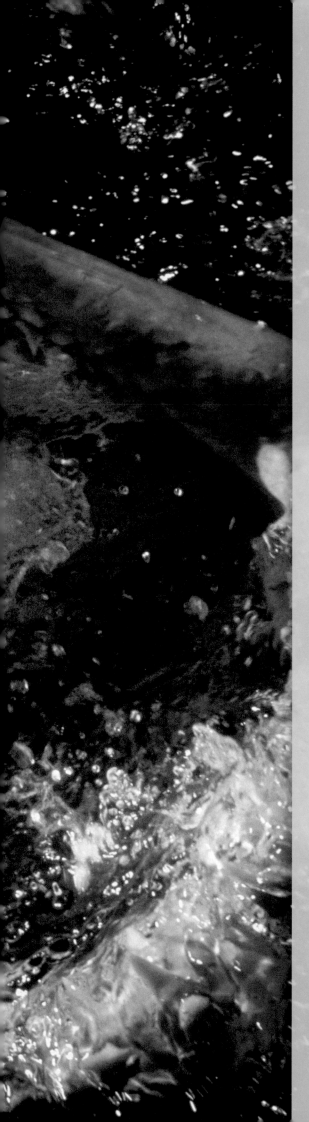

Deadly NATURE

Prepare to be scared—animals are ready to fight tooth and claw when it comes to the crunch, with weapons ranging from lethal toxins to electro-senses.

◀ A great white shark's gaping mouth, lined with daggerlike teeth, looms menacingly upward, ready to engulf potential prey.

Family FEUDS

Family life in the animal world is not all fun and games. There is plenty of motivation for family fights—competition for food is a common source of friction. However, relatives do have their uses, especially when it comes to uniting against a common enemy.

BIRD BRAWL

Given their tendency for violence toward one another, it's a wonder that mallards are one of the most widespread duck species. Life for ducklings is unusually precarious because adults often attack and kill any youngsters they encounter—and some mothers have been known to kill their own offspring in cases of mistaken identity. Drakes (male mallards) also attack each other at breeding time in belligerent battles over territory and mating rights.

A drake may attempt to drown its rival by pinning it below the water.

In Botswana, two bull heads as they attempt to long tusks in a fight for can be so ferocious that

African elephants smash spear each other with their supremacy. Sometimes fights tusks break.

CLASH OF THE TITANS

Brotherly love counts for nothing in an elephant family when it is mating time. Females lead the herds, so when males reach adulthood they are expelled and forced to roam the African plains. Bulls (male elephants) have a reputation as loners, but they often travel with brothers, cousins, or best friends until they come into musth, and their hormones take over. Musth is a frenzied time of fighting when male aggression levels soar, and kinship is forgotten in a competition for mates. It's a conflict that frequently results in serious injury or even death.

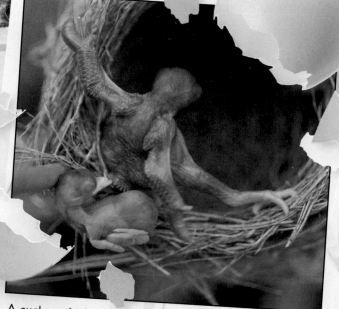

A cuckoo chick ejects its host's chick—a reed warbler—out of the nest, leaving just one mouth to feed—its own!

CUCKOOS IN THE NEST

Bringing up youngsters is risky. For animals, the reward is that their genes are passed onto the next generation. However, sometimes nature plays cruel tricks with caring parents. Cuckoos are brood parasites and lay their eggs in the nests of smaller birds. When the cuckoo chicks hatch, they push the host bird's chicks and eggs out of the nest. Unaware, the host parents continue to raise the cuckoo, which even imitates the "hungry" call of the host's own chicks.

BRINGING UP BABY

There are few animals more dangerous than a mother bear. Once her maternal instincts have been aroused, an adult female with a cub to protect can turn from docile to deadly in seconds. Undaunted by the size of an attacker, mothers will use claws and jaws to fight to the death. They usually only give up when they believe the attacker is dead.

A young brown bear cub looks on as its mother fights off an aggressive male.

Male elephants that are successful in their fights may be able to find as many as 30 mates in just one year, and could father as many calves.

SCHOOL OF HARD KNOCKS

The speed and accuracy required for survival are skills that can take a long time to master, so many youngsters playfight almost as soon as they can walk. Rough and tumble is accompanied by mock punches and gentle bites as siblings develop their hunting and defense strategies.

Young fox cubs playfight with each other until they are around 16 weeks old.

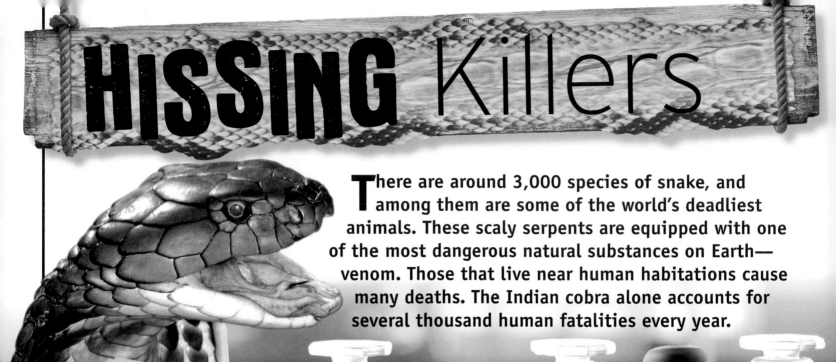

HISSING Killers

There are around 3,000 species of snake, and among them are some of the world's deadliest animals. These scaly serpents are equipped with one of the most dangerous natural substances on Earth— venom. Those that live near human habitations cause many deaths. The Indian cobra alone accounts for several thousand human fatalities every year.

▲ King cobras are the longest venomous snakes in the world, reaching 15 ft (4.6 m) in length.

Rapid elapids

Elapids are a family of snakes that are widespread, and their bite is often deadly to humans. All venomous snakes have fangs, but most elapids have hollow fangs, through which venom flows when the snake bites its victim. Most elapids are slender-bodied, fast movers—black mambas can slither faster than a human can run. A tiny amount of their venom—the weight of a dollar bill—is enough to kill 50 people.

Taipan terror

The taipan, also known as the "fierce snake," possesses one of the most deadly venoms in the world. It targets the nervous system, paralyzing breathing muscles. The snake devours its victim once it is dead. Taipans live in remote regions of Australia, and target lizards, rats, and other small mammals.

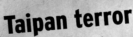

▲ This taipan is ready to strike— one drop of its venom is enough to kill 100 people.

LYSOL

The fangs of a western diamond rattlesnake are covered with a skinlike sheath that pulls back when they are plunged into prey.

Vicious vipers

Vipers have hollow fangs, which, at up to 2 in (5 cm) in length, are much longer than those of elapids. The fangs are hinged, folding away when not in use. Large glands attached to the fangs deliver a venom that attacks the victim's circulatory system, destroying body tissues and muscles. Vipers also have sensory pits on their heads that detect heat given off by prey, allowing them to hunt effectively under the cover of darkness.

ABOUT 600 SNAKE SPECIES ARE VENOMOUS. FEWER THAN ONE THIRD ARE DANGEROUS TO HUMANS.

SQUEEZED TO DEATH

Boas and pythons—constrictors—do not use venom to kill their prey. Instead, they rely on stealth, and their huge size and strength. They can easily kill animals larger than themselves. The secret to their success lies in a constrictor's ability to grip and squeeze. Once it has caught an animal, the snake wraps its muscular coils around it. Each time its victim breathes out, the snake squeezes a little tighter, until the prey finally suffocates.

▼ A python will check each meal's size and shape before working its extending mouth over one end.

PERFECT
Predator

Sharks are awesome hunters of the world's oceans. They have evolved over more then 450 million years to become near-perfect predators. This animal's armory includes: a streamlined body packed with fast-acting muscles, powerful jaws full of razor-sharp teeth, enamel-plated skin, and acute senses.

Ampullae of Lorenzini

Nostril

Eye

Lateral line

A shark uses a variety of senses to pick up information about its environment, both near and far.

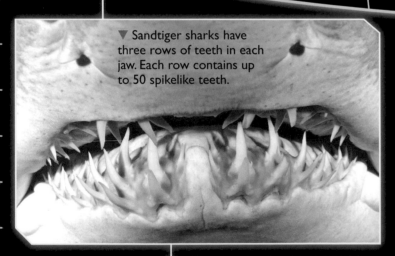

▼ Sandtiger sharks have three rows of teeth in each jaw. Each row contains up to 50 spikelike teeth.

TOOLS FOR THE JOB

A shark's teeth are a guide to its diet. Long, slender, ultrasharp teeth are perfect for gripping slippery squid. Triangular, multi-cusped teeth that look like a saw edge are for carving through flesh and bone. Rows of small, sharp teeth are ideal for grabbing prey from the seabed, and broad, platelike ones can crush the shells of sea turtles.

COOKIE MONSTER

Cookiecutter sharks may be relatively small at just 20 in (50 cm) in length, but they are one of the most savage shark species. A cookiecutter approaches its prey with stealth and speed, then clamps onto its body with its suckerlike mouth, sinking in its rows of sharp teeth. The shark twists its body, making a circular cut, and tears a golf ball-sized plug of flesh away.

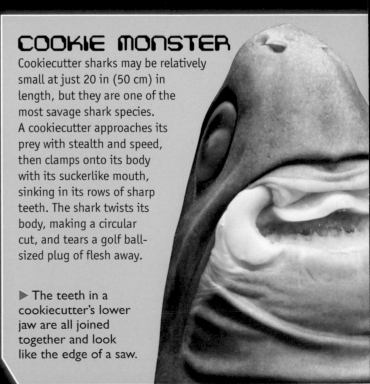

▶ The teeth in a cookiecutter's lower jaw are all joined together and look like the edge of a saw.

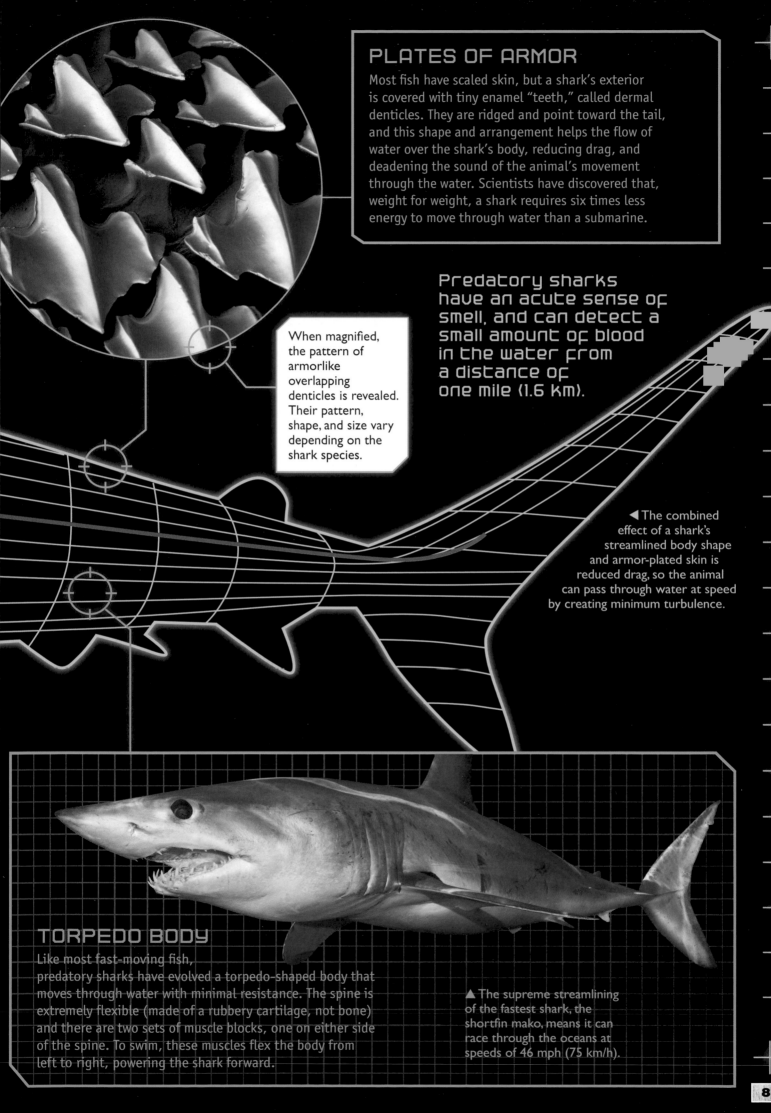

PLATES OF ARMOR

Most fish have scaled skin, but a shark's exterior is covered with tiny enamel "teeth," called dermal denticles. They are ridged and point toward the tail, and this shape and arrangement helps the flow of water over the shark's body, reducing drag, and deadening the sound of the animal's movement through the water. Scientists have discovered that, weight for weight, a shark requires six times less energy to move through water than a submarine.

When magnified, the pattern of armorlike overlapping denticles is revealed. Their pattern, shape, and size vary depending on the shark species.

Predatory sharks have an acute sense of smell, and can detect a small amount of blood in the water from a distance of one mile (1.6 km).

◄ The combined effect of a shark's streamlined body shape and armor-plated skin is reduced drag, so the animal can pass through water at speed by creating minimum turbulence.

TORPEDO BODY

Like most fast-moving fish, predatory sharks have evolved a torpedo-shaped body that moves through water with minimal resistance. The spine is extremely flexible (made of a rubbery cartilage, not bone) and there are two sets of muscle blocks, one on either side of the spine. To swim, these muscles flex the body from left to right, powering the shark forward.

▲ The supreme streamlining of the fastest shark, the shortfin mako, means it can race through the oceans at speeds of 46 mph (75 km/h).

FIGHT-OFF

It is not always easy to predict who will be victorious in a savage encounter in the animal kingdom. Most animals prefer to scare attackers away, rather than engage in a potentially risky fight. However, when opponents do decide to do battle, the winners and losers may come as a surprise.

BUFFALO >>> [DRAW] [DRAW] <<< LION

Brawn vs. brain

African buffaloes are equipped with massive horns, tanklike bodies, thick skin, and bad tempers, so a solo lion's chances of success are low. If the buffalo charges, it will swipe at the lion with its horns, potentially disemboweling the predator with a single movement. Although there may be an initial standoff, no lion would risk pursuing this fight. If a pride of lions manages to isolate a very young, old, or sick buffalo, the outcome might be very different.

SNAKE >>> [WIN] [LOSE] <<< TOAD

Final stand

Confronted by a snake, a soft-bodied toad has few choices. They are slow-moving animals so running isn't an option. Instead, the toad puffs itself up with air, significantly increasing its body size, making it appear a more formidable opponent than it really is and too big for a snake to swallow. Some toads add hissing to the display, and have nasty-tasting skin—but none of these strategies will put off a determined predator, and the toad is unlikely to survive.

BEAR >>> DRAW DRAW <<< WOLF

Dead heat

Wolves are pack hunters that employ sophisticated hunting techniques, while bears mostly rely on a diet of roots, fruits, and berries. Wolves and bears do not normally prey on one another, but they are territorial and protective of their young—traits that can lead to deadly standoffs. Both contenders possess speed, brains, power, and massive jaws. However, although the animals will snarl and bare their teeth for intimidation, the confrontation will end in a draw. Combat would prove too costly for either party, and a face-saving withdrawal is the only sensible option.

SPIDER >>> LOSE WIN! <<< WASP

Spider snacks

Giant tarantula hawk wasps grow as long as a finger, and have powerful stings 0.25 in (6 mm) long. The wasp attacks its tarantula prey by grabbing one of its legs, and, undeterred by the flurry of irritating hairs that the spider hurls, stings its underside. The wasp drags its paralyzed victim into its burrow and lays an egg in its flesh. The newly hatched larva will feast on the still-living spider.

THE VENOMOUS STING OF A TARANTULA HAWK WASP IS EXCRUCIATING AND CAN CAUSE PERMANENT NERVE DAMAGE IN HUMANS.

ARACHNID
Assassins

Arachnids are some of the most successful hunters in the world. Eight nimble legs allow them to leap into action instantly, often seizing their prey before their presence has even been detected. Spiders are arachnids that produce silk—a strong, stretchy thread, perfect for trapping prey—and venom. Fierce-looking scorpions kill with a stabbing stinger.

A net-casting spider holds its web stretched between its legs, ready to snatch any unsuspecting victim below.

Webs, nets, and traps

Orb spiders build typical disk-shaped webs and wait for prey to approach, but net-casting spiders take their web to their prey. Net-casting spiders first spin a small web net. Then, holding it stretched taut between their extra-long front limbs, they leap onto their prey, trapping and wrapping it in silk. Also known as ogre-faced spiders, two of these arachnids' eight eyes are enormous, giving them exceptional night vision.

LETHAL DOSE

Sydney funnelweb spiders combine aggression with powerful venom, making them one of the most dangerous spiders for humans to encounter. They are often found in and around houses and outbuildings in the area around Sydney, Australia. People used to die from the Sydney funnelweb's bite, but since an antivenom was produced in the 1980s, far fewer people have been affected.

◀ The Sydney funnelweb uses its two sharp fangs to strike hard and deliver its potentially lethal dose of venom.

Desert demon

Solifugids may not have stings or venom, but they are fearsome hunters. Their giant fanged, primitive mouthparts are the key to their success. These desert-dwelling arachnids usually grab prey stealthily, or hang from branches during the day. At night, they leave the safety of their dens and go on the rampage, killing large numbers of bugs and spiders, and even larger prey such as rodents and snakes. Their mouthparts can cut through soil and thin bone, slicing a victim's body to pieces in minutes.

◄ A solifugid looks rather like an alien with its bristled face, massive jaws, and beady black eyes.

> SOLIFUGIDS DART TOWARD PREY IN THE BLINK OF AN EYE—THEY CAN RUN 20 IN (50 CM) PER SECOND.

▼ A goldenrod crab spider sinks its fangs into an unsuspecting horsefly.

Crab soup

Crab spiders don't use webs to catch prey. Instead, they lie in wait, expertly camouflaged in their surroundings, to ambush bugs. Some resemble bark, leaves, or bird droppings, while others are brightly colored to match flower petals. A crab spider's venom is strong enough to kill insects bigger than itself. Once a bug has been disabled by a venomous bite, a crab spider will vomit digestive juices onto the victim, so that its tissues dissolve. Then the spider can consume its victim as a "soup."

Sting in the tail

The deathstalker scorpion has a reputation as one of the most dangerous on Earth, even though it is only 3–4 in (7–10 cm) in length. Its claws are small and feeble, but this means it is quick to strike with a sting-bearing tail. The venom is extremely powerful, even in small quantities, and quickly paralyzes a potential meal, or an attacker. To a healthy adult human a deathstalker sting is excruciatingly painful, but its consequences can be far more deadly for a child.

◄ A deathstalker's pincerlike pedipalps (claws) are used to grab prey.

89

ANGRY Birds

Not all birds sit on branches and sing sweetly while eyeing up a juicy berry to eat. Some are born hunters, with weapons to match their savage instincts. Owls and raptors—birds of prey—are notorious, but there are also some unexpected killers in the bird kingdom.

DIVE BOMBER

CLAWED KICKER

Golden eagle
(Aquila chrysaetos)

With a colossal wingspan of up to 7.5 ft (2.3 m) and a top speed of 150 mph (240 km/h), a golden eagle in pursuit of prey is a force to be reckoned with. These raptors dive-bomb their prey, directing a death-blow to the back of the neck. Unlike most raptors, golden eagles often select quarry that are bigger than themselves. The bulk of their diet is made up of small animals such as rabbits and reptiles, but they also attack deer and livestock, including cattle.

Southern cassowary
(Casuarius casuarius)

Cassowaries are large, flightless birds that live in the forests of New Guinea and northeast Australia. They have muscular legs that pack a powerful kick, and, with a 4-in- (10-cm-) long claw on the inside toe of each foot, can inflict a nasty puncture wound. These birds are not hunters, and normally only attack humans to defend themselves or their eggs. They communicate with deep booming calls that are just within the range of human hearing.

Red-backed shrike
(Lanius collurio)

Insect-eating butcherbirds and shrikes have an impressive way to store their food. Once they have caught a small animal or bug, they dispatch it with a vicious peck, and then impale it on a thorn, or barbed wire. This creates a larder that may contain several bugs, small mammals, and reptiles. This gory store of food sustains the birds when they fail to catch anything, and it also impresses potential mates.

BUTCHER BIRD

Secretary bird
(Sagittarius serpentarius)

Long legs help the secretary bird march through the tall grass of the African savanna, stalking prey. These large, slender birds stamp on grass to flush out big insects, small mammals, and snakes to eat. They deliver immense kicks to any animals that bolt, and protect themselves from potentially venomous snake bites by spreading their wings and using them as shields. They can cover more than 19 mi (31 km) in a single day of hunting.

SPEED DEMON

STALKING STAMPER

Ostrich
(Struthio camelus)

Male ostriches usually reserve their aggression for other males, and are swift to attack during the breeding season. They are famous for their bad tempers, so humans and even vehicles are often the focus of ostrich assaults! The tallest, heaviest, and fastest of all birds, the ostrich can reach speeds of more than 43 mph (70 km/h)—and can keep running for an hour or more.

BLOOD Suckers

Animals that feed on blood have a highly specialized way of life, and are usually parasites. Bloodsuckers have a range of ways to pierce skin to get at the protein-packed, nutritious red liquid. Known as hematophagy, feeding on blood is not confined to mosquitoes and vampire bats—some species of bird, fish, moth, and other bugs also enjoy a bloody feast.

A TICK FEEDING ON AN ANIMAL VICTIM

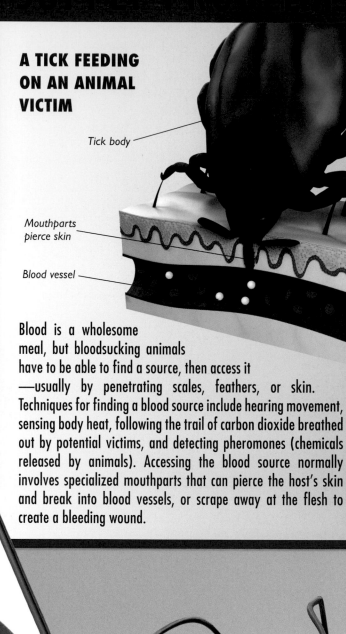

Tick body

Mouthparts pierce skin

Blood vessel

Blood is a wholesome meal, but bloodsucking animals have to be able to find a source, then access it —usually by penetrating scales, feathers, or skin. Techniques for finding a blood source include hearing movement, sensing body heat, following the trail of carbon dioxide breathed out by potential victims, and detecting pheromones (chemicals released by animals). Accessing the blood source normally involves specialized mouthparts that can pierce the host's skin and break into blood vessels, or scrape away at the flesh to create a bleeding wound.

Hungry mothers

Female mosquitoes must feed on the protein and iron found in blood before they can lay eggs. The fly's syringelike mouthpart—a proboscis—pierces skin and delivers anticoagulants as blood is sucked up, to stop clotting. Each mosquito takes a tiny amount of blood, but the damage to the victim lies in the deadly microorganisms that these bugs often leave behind. Mosquitoes can transmit diseases such as malaria, dengue fever, yellow fever, and encephalitis.

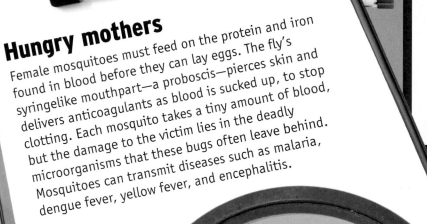

▶ Worldwide research continues into the problem of deadly diseases that are transmitted by mosquitoes.

Sucker fish

Sea lampreys are parasitic jawless fish that mostly feed on other fish and marine mammals. They attach to their victims with suckerlike mouths lined with rows of horny teeth that scrape away at the flesh. As they feed, lampreys douse the wound with anticoagulants. Once its stomach is full, the lamprey disengages its mouth from the victim and falls away, leaving a gaping, bleeding wound.

▶ Lampreys become parasites when they are adults, and use their circular, toothed mouths to latch onto fish, such as trout (inset). They feed until they are ready to mate and die after their eggs are laid.

DRACULA BATS

Vampire bats have powerful hind legs and unusually strong thumbs that help them crawl and clamber onto a victim.

Vampires really do exist, but these bats scarcely deserve the gruesome reputation they have acquired since the first stories of Dracula. Most species of vampire bat feed on the blood of cows and horses, not humans. Vampire bats need to consume about two tablespoons of blood a day—more than half of their body weight. They have pit organs on their faces that are covered with heat-detecting molecules to sense body heat. Furtive vampire bats crawl on the ground to approach their prey, and sink their ultrasharp fangs into a spot where blood is close to the surface. They produce a chemical that reduces pain, and keeps the blood flowing as they lap.

93

TEETH and JAWS

MAXIMUM ANIMAL BITE FORCES
Figures are estimates, shown in Newtons (N)

Carcharodon megalodon
(extinct giant shark) 182,200 N

Tyrannosaurus rex 60,000 N

Great white shark 17,790 N

Saltwater crocodile 16,460 N

Dunkleosteus terrelli
(extinct marine fish) 5,000 N

African lion 4,500 N

Hyena 2,000 N

Human 890 N

Tasmanian devil
553 N

About 430 to 445 million years ago the first jawed animals evolved. Their jaws developed from gill arches—the bony parts that support a fish's gill slits. Jaws allowed fish to become hunters rather than just being passive eaters. Today, predators show a range of highly specialized jaws and teeth that can grab, squash, pierce, grind, slice, slash, and mash.

▼ *Dunkleosteus* lived about 360 million years ago.

▼ A lioness in Botswana uses her carnassial teeth to shear flesh from a buffalo carcass.

JAWS OF THE DEEP

The prehistoric seas were home to *Dunkleosteus*, a giant sharklike fish with bizarre structures for biting. Instead of teeth, *Dunkleosteus* had large bony blades in its jaws, which could slice effectively. They were capable of crushing bone—*Dunkleosteus* had the second strongest bite of any fish—and turning fish prey into mincemeat in minutes. This marine monster was protected from attack by an armor-plated skull.

Carnivore club

Meat-eating predators, such as lions, have skulls packed with large muscles and outsize teeth. This allows the jaw to exert a massive bite force with incredible grip. The upper and lower jaw are connected by a hinge joint that allows movement vertically only. Supersized temporalis muscles that operate the jaws are so large that they make up most of the bulk of a lion's head. Carnivore canine teeth are enlarged, sharp, and pointed for piercing flesh, while scissorlike carnassial teeth that line the sides of the jaws shred and shear flesh.

▶ A hyena's teeth are larger than average for its body size, especially the bone-crushing premolars and shearing molars.

Fearless and ferocious

Hyenas are reputed to have the most powerful jaws of any mammal for their body size, and they can crack bone with ease. These strong mammals are aggressive virtually from birth and often hunt in groups. There have been attacks recorded on people camping in hyena territory—campers have awoken to find hyena jaws clamped onto their limbs, taking mouthfuls of flesh in an instant.

Open wide

Hippopotamuses hold a reputation as one of the most dangerous animals in Africa. Despite their exclusively herbivorous diet, these large mammals are extremely aggressive. A hippo's fervent instinct to protect itself, its young, and its territory means an encounter with one may prove fatal. Weighing in at 1.5 tons, with giant pointed tusks that measure 20 in (50 cm) in length, and jaws that can open to nearly 180 degrees, this grass-eater is no gentle giant.

◀ A bull hippo fights other males to protect his mating rights over a harem of up to 30 females.

Double trouble

Moray eels can keep hold of slippery prey thanks to a second set of jaws deep inside their throats. Rows of razor-sharp teeth in the front jaws clench hold of a fish while the rear jaws shoot forward into the mouth. Lined with bigger teeth, these jaws clamp down, and pull the fish down the eel's esophagus and toward its stomach.

▶ Most fish "suck" prey into their throats, but moray eels use their second jaws instead.

Front jaws and teeth

Pharyngeal jaws (rear extendable jaws)

95

PAWS and Claws

Powerful paws and lacerating claws are key weapons, allowing an animal to inflict injury while keeping its own head out of the line of fire. Clawed paws are often specialized, with features that have evolved to match the hunting requirements of their owner.

SPURS OF VENOM

The duck-billed platypus is one of very few types of venomous mammal in the world. Only males possess a curved claw, or spur, on each of their hind legs. These spurs are attached to glands that release venom. Males only use their spurs when kicking out at their natural enemies and other males, especially at mating time.

▶ A platypus's venom is not deadly to humans, but it is said to cause intense pain.

◀ A polar bear's huge paws can be up to 12 in (30 cm) in diameter.

Polar paws

Polar bears are the largest carnivores on land, and they have huge paws to match. In their Arctic habitat, broad paws act like snowshoes, spreading the polar bear's weight on snow and thin ice. They also help the bears to stalk their seal prey—tufts of fur between the toes deaden the noise of their step. Short, stout, curved claws pierce and rip flesh easily, and can haul a seal out of an ice hole to eat.

Indian devils

Wolverines may be no bigger than dogs, but these fearless creatures attack bears and deer, earning them the alternative name of "Indian devil." They are weasel-like mammals that live in northern regions where polar conditions leave predators hungry, desperate, and fearless. A wolverine's paws are large, flat, and furry with broad pads and very long claws. They are perfect for chasing down prey over deep snow, and holding onto a victim while the wolverine delivers a neck-breaking bite with its immensely powerful jaws.

▶ Wolverines both hunt and scavenge, feasting on any animal they can find.

▲ At rest, the hairy frog doesn't look special, but its hidden weapon makes potential attackers think twice.

Snap claws

In the natural world, fact can be stranger than fiction. When threatened, African hairy frogs snap the bones in their feet. The broken bones rip through the skin, jutting out as knifelike extensions on the frog's fingertips and toes. This gives them an effective set of razor-sharp claws to swipe at an attacker.

Crushing coconuts

When Charles Darwin encountered the world's largest land-living species of crab on the Keeling Islands, he described it as "monstrous." These land-living crustaceans, which are known as robber or coconut crabs, have a legspan of up to 40 in (one meter). Coconut crabs feed mainly on fruit, and their name comes from their ability to open the tough shells of coconuts. Occasionally they use their enormous claws to attack other crabs, and they have been known to turn cannibal and eat their fallen opponent after a fight.

A coconut crab's strong claws can easily pull its body up a tree to reach the fruit at the top.

CRABS HAVE ONE OF THE GREATEST CLAW FORCES FOR BODY SIZE IN THE ANIMAL KINGDOM.

Feline FIENDS

Cats are famous for their killing skills—their supreme strength and elegance combine to create a sublime predator. Cats all share the same basic body features. They have short muzzles equipped with wide-opening jaws, sharp fangs, and meat-shearing carnassial teeth. They also all have highly developed senses, powerful limbs, and paws that are tooled with retractable claws.

◄ A lioness keeps low to the ground as she stalks prey at dusk.

STEALTH

1

Few animals can stalk their prey with the stealth of a cat. Colored or patterned fur helps a cat to remain hidden in undergrowth as it chooses and follows a potential victim. A characteristic crawl, with its body close to the ground, allows the predator to creep closer—its unblinking eyes fixed and focused on the prey. Leopards move so quietly that they have been known to pluck a sleeping human victim from their bed and escape without a sound—the room's other occupants only find out about the midnight visitor the next morning.

SPEED

2

Felines are able to accelerate fast but, unlike members of the dog family, are unable to sustain a chase for long. Cheetahs are the swiftest of all land animals over short distances. A very narrow body, slender limb bones, almost vertical shoulder blades, and a flexible spine mean this cat is not just streamlined, it can make enormous energy-efficient strides. However, at high speeds the cat gets so hot that it cannot run further than about 1,600 ft (500 m) during a chase before risking death from overheating.

POUNCE

► A caracal's long, strong back legs are perfect for running down speedy prey such as hares and antelopes.

ONE FEARLESS LEOPARD IN INDIA WAS PROBABLY RESPONSIBLE FOR MORE THAN 125 HUMAN DEATHS IN JUST TEN YEARS.

THE FEAR FACTOR

When an animal knows a big cat is nearby, the fear factor takes over. Their body goes into a state of stress, ready to run or defend itself—the "fight or flight" response. Adrenaline courses through the blood vessels, increasing the rate of blood circulation, breathing, metabolism of carbohydrates, and preparing the muscles for exertion. Although felines are superb predators, most of their potential victims escape unharmed.

▲ A gazelle bounds away from its hunter —the big cat.

◀ Mid-chase, a cheetah lowers its head for extra streamlining, and extends its claws for a better grip on the ground.

Leaping and pouncing skills give a feline the advantage of surprise. Prey may have judged their stalker to be at a safe distance, only to be shocked, seconds later, to find a fanged set of jaws looming overhead. Snow leopards hold the record for the longest recorded leap of any cat, at 49 ft (15 m), but caracals and servals are the bounciest cats. Pouncing enables a cat to approach its prey from above, which means it can avoid potential bites and scratches while delivering a lethal blow.

3

In the final stages of a hunt, cats employ speed and strength and go for the throat. With their jaws tightly clamped around the windpipe, a cat effectively suffocates its prey, and the victim usually suffers a quick death. Large cats can hunt prey bigger than themselves, and often drag their victim to a safe location before settling down to eat.

▼ A jaguar clamps its strong jaws onto the skull of an unfortunate caiman.

4

SLAUGHTER

BRUTAL Bugs

▶ A tailless whip scorpion begins to munch through the body of a grasshopper.

You don't have to be big to be brutal. Skulking beneath rocks, lurking in the undergrowth, flitting through the air, and even hiding in our homes there is an almost invisible world of mini-monsters, battling it out for survival.

Acid attack

Giant vinegaroons resemble a cross between a scorpion and a spider, and share some of the most savage characteristics of both. These arachnids—also known as whip scorpions—grab their invertebrate victims with their heavy, armored pedipalps and crush them to death. They deter predators by bombarding them with a noxious spray that is 84 percent acid.

▼ Bulldog ants are only found in Australia. They live in colonies but forage and hunt alone—mostly feeding on smaller carpenter ants.

▼ Capable of killing 40 honeybees in a minute, this giant hornet kills more people in Japan every year than any other animal.

Nonstop stingers

Ants are brutal bugs with vicious stings—they belong to the same family as bees, wasps, and hornets. Bullet ants are named for their stings, which are said to feel like a gunshot, and fire ants hold tight to an attacker and keep stinging for as long as they can. Bulldog ants are fierce, but one look at their menacing jaws should be enough to scare any attacker away.

Big, bold, and bad

In Japan, Asian giant hornets are called sparrow-wasps because at 2 in (5 cm) in length, they look similar to small birds when in flight. Like other members of the bee and wasp family, these insects administer pain-inducing stings, but they also inject a neurotoxin that can prove lethal. Thankfully they usually reserve their aggression for colonies of honeybees rather than people.

▶ The moon moth caterpillar uses both camouflage and toxic spines to defend itself.

Death by caterpillar

It is hard to believe that soft-bodied, plant-eating caterpillars could inflict a potentially fatal wound on any creature, yet some caterpillars have been known to kill humans. Lonomia caterpillars gather together in large groups, on the ground, or in trees. They are covered in detachable hairy spines that deliver powerful chemicals that burn, and cause swelling, headaches, and blisters. Within 12 hours the worst possible symptom may occur— the victim slowly bleeds to death.

Creepy-crawly killer

People living in the southwestern region of the United States fear the giant centipede *Scolopendra heros*, with good reason. These invertebrates can grow to 8 in (20 cm) in length and inflict an incredibly painful bite, thanks to the venom that all centipedes possess. Larger centipedes can deliver more venom with each bite, so the Amazonian giant centipede—which grows to 12 in (30 cm) long—is best avoided.

◀ Giant centipedes mostly hunt other invertebrates, such as beetles and flies, but they also feed on birds, mice, lizards, and frogs.

Cold-blooded KILLERS

Most reptiles and amphibians are active hunters. These are ancient groups of animals that have developed a diverse range of hunting techniques. There are cannibalistic "dragons," sit-and-wait predators, stalking crocodilians, slimy salamanders, and even frogs with fangs.

CAUTION: Surinam horned frog

Surinam horned frogs are expert ambushers. Their peculiar flattened appearance allows these large amphibians to partly bury themselves in the ground and remain undetected by prey. When victims approach, the frogs leap into action. Unusually for frogs, they have toothlike bony projections from the jaw, so they immobilize their prey with a single bite before swallowing it whole.

▶ A Surinam horned frog may sit absolutely still for several days, waiting for lunch—such as a bullfrog—to pass by.

DANGER: Nile crocodile

Many savage animals only resort to aggression when provoked, or in self-defense. However, crocodiles almost always attack with a single purpose in mind—getting a meal. Most crocodiles ambush their prey, and typically attack at the water's edge. They lunge forward, take a strong hold with their jaws, and pull the victim underwater. Once there, they will roll around in the water, which can disorientate prey, drown it, and snap its spine.

◀ A crocodile's eyes, ears, and nose are all on top of its head, so that it can lie in wait for prey almost completely submerged.

THE KILLER QUESTION

A mystery surrounds the savage lifestyle of *Tyrannosaurus rex*. While this dinosaur certainly had the appearance of a ferocious predator, scientists argue that it may have been more of a scavenger. They argue that its hind limbs would have been far too heavy for fast running, and that those feeble forearms would not have been much use in grabbing prey. It has also been suggested that *T rex* was a cannibal and had lethal bacteria in its saliva, like the Komodo dragon of today.

WARNING: Komodo dragon

The Lesser Sunda Islands in Indonesia are so remote that the existence of their now most famous inhabitants was widely unknown until 100 years ago. Komodo dragons are the largest living lizards, reaching 10 ft (3 m) in length. They combine a monstrous appearance with a savage nature—feeding on almost anything, and attacking large animals, including humans. Adult Komodos will also eat younger members of their own species, so youngsters often have to hide in trees to avoid being eaten.

▼ An antelope's leg disappears down a dragon's gaping throat—an adult Komodo can eat up to 80 percent of its own body weight at one time.

HAZARD: Japanese giant salamander

Salamanders are amphibians, like frogs and toads, but with tails. They are all carnivores, but they can withstand long periods without any food at all. Many are dull-colored for camouflage but fire salamanders have bold yellow markings to warn that they produce a toxic substance. Japanese giant salamanders grow to almost 5 ft (1.5 m). They have slimy, mucus-covered skin and huge mouths. They lie in wait for food to pass by and grab prey with an almighty snap of their jaws.

◀ At night a Japanese giant salamander is alert, but in the day it rests beneath rocks.

RIVER SAFARI

Under the still surface of a lake or the gently rippling waters of a river, undiscovered assassins lurk. Although humans have been using waterways for many thousands of years, the waters still hide many savage secrets. We are only just beginning to understand what an incredible wealth of fascinating animal stories the world's rivers have to tell.

Mystery monster

Giant freshwater stingrays are among the world's biggest river killers. At half the length of a bus, they are strong enough to pull boats along rivers or underwater. Giant stingrays remained undiscovered until the 1990s and new species are now being identified in Indo-Pacific river regions. Stingrays are usually passive fish, but they may attack people who try to handle them. Their tails have arrowlike barbs of up to 15 in (38 cm) that can break through skin and penetrate bone to deliver deadly venom.

▼ Despite their awesome size, giant stingrays are difficult to find, catch, or study.

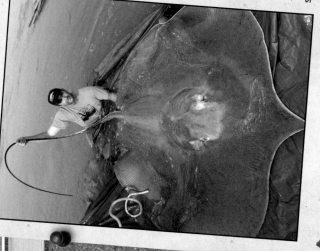

Big, bad bugs

Giant water bugs are the largest insect river monsters in the world. They can walk, fly, and swim, using their wings to store air while they hunt underwater. These huge aquatic insects sit motionless waiting for prey to approach them, then make a grab with pincerlike front legs. Needlelike mouthparts inject saliva into the victim, and its body juices are sucked out.

Water bugs have been observed eating baby turtles, and even snakes.

Man-eating catfish

Tales of man-eating catfish have been around for centuries, and the wels catfish is often named as the number one suspect. These massive fish are certainly equipped to kill, with huge jaws lined with hundreds of small teeth and an aggressive temperament at mating time. While this fish may pose some risk to humans, its natural prey are much smaller—crustaceans, fish, frogs, worms, and ducks.

▲ Little is known about these monster fish, so explorer Zeb Hogan has launched a project to protect them and other freshwater giants.

Survival strategy

The alligator gar is a menacing megafish with a long, toothed snout. It preys on fish, turtles, and birds. The gar's eggs and yolk sacs have a very unusual feature that has doubtless helped these ancient fish to survive—they are toxic to crustaceans and many vertebrates. Crayfish and blue crabs are especially vulnerable to the poison, and even humans are affected just by handling alligator gar eggs.

▶ An alligator gar can grow to 10 ft (3 m) in length and gets its name from its long, toothy snout.

Wels catfish use their barbels (whiskerlike sense organs) to taste, and feel their way in murky water.

With its dull colors and strange body shape, an alligator snapping turtle has perfect camouflage.

WIGGLING, WRIGGLING WORMS

A primitive beast lurks in the murky waters of swamps in the southeastern states of the U.S.—the alligator snapping turtle. This ancient animal demonstrates an impressive hunting trick—it lies with its jaws wide open to expose a red wriggling structure on its tongue, which looks like a worm. Fish are tempted into the monster's beaklike mouth, which then slams shut.

SMASH! BANG! WALLOP!

Gripping jaws, **snipping** teeth, **Gripping** claws—for some animals these standard tools of **savagery** are far too predictable. They use rather more surprising techniques to overpower their enemies, and get their point across in style.

Male strawberry poison frogs prefer to wrestle in the mornings. In the afternoon they eat, mate, and look after their young.

Two whitetail deer bucks square up for battle. Extra-thick skulls help protect their brains from the damaging effects of a smashing time.

CRUNCH!

GRAPPLE!

For a male antelope or deer, the rewards for fighting are high and the winner takes it all. These animals operate harems, which means one male can win mating rights over a whole group of females, ensuring that future generations will carry his genes. In some species of antelope, horns can grow to 5 ft (1.5 m) in length—and particularly impressive horns may help a male to assert his dominance over other males without the need for fighting. However, if a fight-off is necessary, the stakes are high. Broken horns are a common injury following head-butting clashes, but others can be far more life-threatening.

Male strawberry poison frogs are proud homeowners, but they only welcome guests of the female kind. A male spends the morning warning neighboring males to keep their distance, but if one does stray over the invisible boundary a flesh-on-flesh battle will follow. The males hold tight and wrestle to the ground, pushing one another with their strong legs—the loser is forced to the ground and must leave the area in shame.

POISON FROGS HAVE FEW ENEMIES, AS THEIR COLORFUL SKIN IS HIGHLY TOXIC.

PUNCH!

Hooved animals can use brute force to demolish any opposition. A fast kick delivers bone-crunching force, which is why horses and zebras are animals to be respected. Zebra stallions fight over mating rights and feeding grounds. In the first instance a small kick may be enough to persuade rivals to move, but if that doesn't work a stallion may deliver a series of deadly blows, usually aimed at a rival's head.

THWACK!

Male Eastern gray kangaroos fight at mating time, but these sparring skills are also useful for battling dingos (wild dogs).

Kangaroos are famous for their kickboxing skills. These marsupial bruisers put everything into a confrontation—jabbing with clawed forepaws, grappling, and delivering mighty kicks from muscular hindlegs.

It takes great strength and agility for a zebra to launch an attack, but for the victor this vicious battle will be worth the effort.

When males of almost any species square up to each other, there is a show of size and strength. Male swans raise their bodies out of the water, spread their wings and curve their necks—and the smaller bird may turn tail at this point. If not, a vicious battle may follow and can result in death. Wings and beaks are used as weapons.

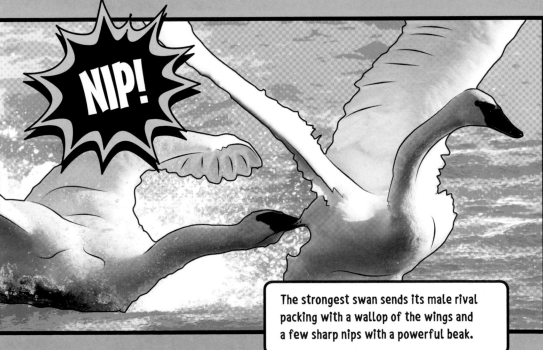

NIP!

The strongest swan sends its male rival packing with a wallop of the wings and a few sharp nips with a powerful beak.

COOL, CRUEL World

L ife in the extreme habitats of the Arctic and Antarctic poses particular problems for wildlife. Without warmth and light to support much plant growth on land, most of the animals that survive here have to be meat or fish eaters. The outcome of a hunt may spell life or death when the next meal may be many miles, or days, away.

White wanderer

The Arctic fox hunts and scavenges a wide variety of prey depending on its location.

Foxes are among the most successful mammals in the world, and are able to survive in a huge variety of habitats. Arctic foxes exemplify this success because they have impressive adaptations to seasonal extremes in the north. During the summer, their brown coats provide camouflage in woodlands and scrub, but in the winter they grow very thick white pelts, and take shelter in huge underground dens with extensive burrow systems.

A parasitic copepod is just visible, attached to this Greenland shark's eye.

Ice shark

Ancient, slow-moving assassins live beneath the Arctic ice. Greenland sharks are the second-largest carnivorous sharks in the world. They only grow 0.5 in (one centimeter) per year, so a 20 ft (6 m) individual may be centuries old. Young Greenland sharks are likely to prey upon seals. Older individuals often have to scavenge, after parasites attack their eyes, making them blind.

AVIAN THUG

Arctic skuas have a huge range, and spend their summers along northern coasts of America and Europe. They are also known as parasitic jaegers.

Arctic skuas are kleptoparasites (food thieves), predators, and scavengers. One tactic is to threaten other birds until they regurgitate food, which the skua then eats. They attack smaller birds, and even dive-bomb large animals, including humans. Most onslaughts are aerial attacks, but some skuas have been seen sneaking up on nesting colonies of Arctic terns on foot. This approach fools the terns, which did not notice their eggs and chicks being stolen until too late.

ARCTIC ASSASSIN

Polar bears are the biggest and most ruthless of all bears. Their immense bodies are packed with muscles and fat, and they require an energy-rich diet to keep warm, and to power their predatory lifestyles. One bear needs to kill up to 75 seals per year to survive, but can live for up to eight months without feeding. Polar bears are one of the few predators that are known to hunt humans actively for food, although females are most dangerous when they are protecting their cubs.

Polar bear mothers teach their cubs to hunt. These cubs are fighting over whale meat.

This king penguin's nasty wound was inflicted by a leopard seal.

KING PENGUINS CAN GO FOR MONTHS BETWEEN MEALS. ONE CHICK SURVIVED FOR FIVE MONTHS WITHOUT EATING.

Snowy survivor

Penguins only feed in the sea, and can hunt their prey of fish at top speeds of 22 mph (35 km/h), appearing to almost fly through the water. Emperor penguins dive to depths of at least 1,740 ft (530 m) to reach fish, crustaceans, and squid. These birds have sharp-edged, hooked bills and their throats and tongues are coated with backward-pointing spines—features that ensure captured fish are on a one-way route to the stomach. Penguins face predation from seabirds, such as skuas, and leopard seals. One leopard seal may devour 12 Adélie penguins for a single meal.

DEATH SQUAD

There is not only safety in numbers—there is power. When animals work together to hunt and kill, they become a deadly force. Combining efforts means a successful hunt is more likely, and everyone gets a share of the kill. These death squads of the natural world have little to fear from predators or prey.

WOLVES ARE PACK ANIMALS. THEY CAN SMELL PREY MORE THAN 1.2 MI (2 KM) AWAY AND HEAR SOUNDS UP TO 6 MI (10 KM) AWAY.

Lion's share

A pride of lions can dominate the landscape, invoking panic among nearby herds of herbivores. When it is time to feed, the primary hunters—the females—become more furtive. They stalk and surround their prey, constantly checking one another's position, before launching into the attack. Working together they can fell big prey, killing by sinking their teeth into the victim's windpipe, causing suffocation.

TWO LIONESSES WORK TOGETHER TO BACK A WILDEBEEST INTO A CORNER AND PREPARE TO STRIKE.

Canny canids

Many dog species combine superb senses with cooperation, communication, and a strong social structure. African hunting dogs exemplify the canid lifestyle. They live in packs led by a dominant breeding pair, and hunt in groups of six to 20 animals. Their methods are brutal but efficient, pursuing a victim until it almost collapses with exhaustion, and taking opportunistic bites of flesh during the chase.

A PACK OF DOGS TARGETS A LONE WARTHOG, AND THE VICTIM DISAPPEARS ALMOST INSTANTLY IN THE FEEDING FRENZY.

Killer whales

It has recently been discovered that orcas (killer whales) hunt in cooperative groups. These intelligent, adaptable animals will herd fish toward each other and then stun them with blows from their tail flukes. Against seals they employ a strategy known as "wave-hunting." Their ability to learn is key to their success—young orcas watch the hunt, and learn the technique.

1

WAVE-HUNTING

1. AT FIRST, THE GROUP OF ORCAS RAISE THEIR HEADS OUT OF THE WATER TO LOOK FOR SEALS RESTING ON ICE FLOES.

2

2. HAVING IDENTIFIED A TARGET, THE ORCAS SWIM AS A GROUP TOWARD AND BENEATH THE FLOE.

3

3. THIS CREATES A WAVE OR SWELL LARGE ENOUGH TO ROCK OR TIP THE FLOE, CAUSING THE SEAL TO FALL OFF THE ICE AND INTO THE ORCAS' WAITING MOUTHS.

SUPER

POWERS

In the animal world, fantastical creatures and astounding stories of survival and savagery abound. From the murky bottom of the seabed to the dark interior of an insect's nest there are battles to be fought and won—and some of them involve extraordinary powers.

Little pistol shrimps may not look very impressive but these tiny marine crustaceans have a super power that packs a sonic punch. One claw is much bigger than the other—and this is the shrimp's secret weapon. As the claw is snapped shut a jet of water fires out at 60 mph (100 km/h), creating a bubble of superheated air in its wake. The bubble bursts, creating a loud cracking sound and a flash of light. The bang is powerful enough to stun, or even kill, prey.

CRACK!

Pistol Shrimp

A cuckoo wasp is able to infiltrate the nest of a beewolf (another type of wasp), lay its eggs, and escape—all without being detected. It achieves this incredible feat by means of an invisibility "cloak." The cuckoo wasp's skin is coated in chemicals that mimic the beewolf's own skin so closely that the beewolf thinks it is playing host to a member of its own family, not a trespasser. When the cuckoo wasp's eggs hatch, the larvae devour the beewolf's offspring.

SNEAK!

Cuckoo Wasp

BOXER CRAB

KAPOW!

Small boxer crabs employ even tinier friends to help them become more brutal. They hold stinging sea anemones in their pincers and wave them about, like a boxer brandishing his gloved fists. By waving the anemones, the little pugilists show possible attackers that they are armed and ready. In return, the anemones feed on the crab's leftovers.

BOMBARDIER BEETLE

SQUIRT!

An explosive force can be a highly effective weapon, and animals knew this long before Alfred Nobel invented dynamite! Bombardier beetles combine liquids in their bodies to create a hot, toxic, and explosive liquid that they can aim at predators with incredible accuracy. Bombardier beetles are not the only insects to employ explosive defense methods: kamikaze termites and ants spontaneously rupture their bodies to release a toxic flare if their colony is in danger—but at least these bugs go out with a bang!

All animals have electricity in their bodies, but few have turned a normal life function into a killing force. Discharging electricity is called electrogenesis and electric eels are masters of the art. Despite their name these animals are not true eels, but a type of long-bodied fish, called a knifefish. Using up to 6,000 special "battery" cells on its abdomen, an electric eel can generate and store 600 volts, which it uses to stun or kill its prey.

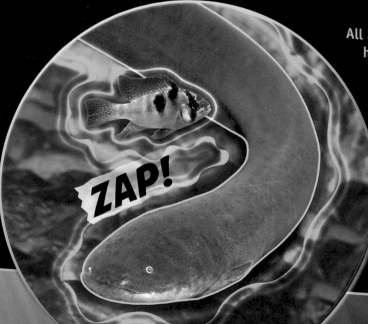

ZAP!

ELECTRIC EEL

Amazing NATURE

Take a closer look at the must-see moments and breathtaking drama of spectacular events in the wild.

◀ Perched on the edge of a waterfall, a grizzly bear carefully balances as salmon fling themselves out of the water and into its menacing jaws.

PENGUINS
on Parade

The life of an emperor penguin demands powers of endurance far beyond our grasp. During the extremes of a polar winter, these flightless birds undertake extraordinary treks to rear their chicks and find food. They suffer starvation and endure bone-chilling blizzards in subzero temperatures.

▼ Up to 5,000 males huddle together, taking turns in the middle of the group where it is warmest.

▼ There is no nest, so the male warms the egg against a patch of bare belly skin.

Buddy body warmth
While the females feast on fish and squid, storing energy as body fat, the males huddle together for warmth and wait. Blisteringly cold winds whip around the colony. Far from the sea, the males cannot feed, and survive on stores of body fat. It will be around 64 days until the females return.

Meeting a mate
With little land in the Southern Ocean, emperor penguins must wait for sea ice to form in early winter before they can leave the water and set off on the long journey across the pack ice to the breeding colonies. Here they form pairs, and the female lays a single egg in mid-May. She transfers her egg onto its father's broad feet, and departs for the sea. He will care for the egg until she returns.

EMPEROR PENGUINS HAVE MULTIPLE LAYERS OF SCALELIKE FEATHERS THAT ARE TIGHTLY PACKED, SO ONLY THE HARSHEST WINDS CAN RUFFLE THEM.

▼ An emperor penguin can dive to depths of 1,300 ft (400 m), staying underwater for up to 20 minutes.

In their element

Upon their return to the sea, the emperors' clumsy movements on land become a distant memory. Their torpedo-shaped bodies cut through the water at up to 9 mph (around 14 km/h), and they can dive to depths where there is little or no light. No one knows how the birds find their prey in deep water that is as dark as ink.

▼ Crossing vast expanses of ice is hard work, so penguins toboggan on their bellies to save energy.

▶ Parents protect their chicks from the extreme cold and predators, such as skuas.

From fast to feast

The males must now undertake a journey of up to 60 mi (100 km) across the ice to reach open water. After feeding they return to the colony and from then on, both parent birds take turns hunting to feed their chick. When the sea ice begins to break up at the height of summer, the chicks and adults journey to the sea to forage.

Single parents

Fully fed, the females arrive back at the colony in time for the hatching of the eggs. Each male hands over his egg and heads off seaward. When the egg hatches, the chick is fed by the mother with regurgitated food.

LEAP of Faith

Ocean-swimming salmon head inland to breed and the sheer number of fish surging upriver makes for a captivating spectacle. For greedy grizzlies, however, this is a flying feast of fast-moving, protein-packed lunches—and an opportunity to enjoy some freshwater fishing.

Fast food

In summer, sockeye salmon begin the journey home—they must spawn (lay their eggs) in the rivers where they themselves hatched. Knowing a feast is on its way, grizzly bears gather by rapids and falls where the salmon leap out of the water to travel upstream, or plunge into the river to trap the fish against the river floor with their giant paws. A summer diet of salmon enables a grizzly to store enough fat to survive the winter, when it may eat very little for months.

PROTEIN PACKS

Scientists once believed there were different species of brown bear. DNA tests, however, have proved they are all the same and they share the species name of *Ursus arctos*. The variance in sizes is mostly due to the bears' diets. Kodiak bears and coastal grizzlies have access to high-protein diets.

Kodiak
4.5 ft (1.4 m)

Coastal Grizzly
4 ft (1.2 m)

Inland Grizzly
3.5 ft (1.1 m)

Subspecies to scale (height at shoulder)

▶ In some places, the fish are so numerous that a bear merely has to stand with its mouth open to catch a salmon as it flings itself through the air.

Need to breed

As they travel, the salmon change from silvery blue to bright red, with greenish heads. The color develops in their skins, not their scales (which are transparent) and signifies that they are ready to mate. Ten million sockeyes may migrate up just one river in a single spawning season, turning sections of the watercourse into a cauldron of thrashing scarlet bodies. These salmon will never make the journey again—they reproduce only once in their lives.

▲ The salmon swim upstream and the females search for a suitable place to lay their eggs in the gravel, in hollows called redds.

▶ The salmon die, but their rotting bodies return nutrients to the habitat, helping to feed the fry (young fish) and other animals in the river.

Onward and upward

The salmon hordes soldier on, but their numbers fall with every grizzly onslaught. Eventually, the survivors reach the upstream gravel beds. Females release their eggs while the males fertilize them. Soon both parents will die.

Hatch and go

After several months the eggs will hatch, and the fry stay in the river until the following summer. As young adults they begin the reverse migration, heading downstream to the ocean.

▶ A newly hatched sockeye is called an alevin. It stays in its redd for a month, and survives on food in the egg's yolk.

Butterfly CLOUDS

Many birds make incredible journeys, but how do tiny, fragile insects survive monumental migrations of 2,000 mi (around 3,000 km)? Monarch butterflies head south for winter, but their epic odyssey is just one part of a bizarre life cycle.

▶ Each monarch adult has a long, slender proboscis (sucking mouthpart), which absorbs liquid nectar from inside the flower.

Generation X

Every year, the final summer generation of North American monarch adults (imagos) is different to those that came before. Instead of a short and predictable life spent sipping nectar and reproducing, these daredevils are fated to start the long journey to Mexico. As days shorten and the cool autumn air sweeps in, these imagos feed, store their energy, and set off.

METAMORPHOSIS

Butterflies undergo metamorphosis, transforming from caterpillars into their adult form. During the summer, the caterpillars feed on milkweed, storing its toxic, milky sap in their bodies and becoming poisonous to potential predators.

1. Fat, mature caterpillars pupate. During this time of metamorphosis their bodies will develop into adults, or imagos.

2. The pupa is suspended by a silken thread. Body parts, such as the wings and abdomen, are visible on the pupa.

3. An adult emerges from the pupa. Its body is still soft and will have to harden before the imago can fly.

A multitude of monarchs

Using the Sun as a compass and Earth's magnetic field to navigate, millions of imagos instinctively fly south. Feeding en route, the monarchs actually gain weight on their journey—possibly saving energy by gliding on air currents. They cluster together at night to rest.

▼ Countless monarchs take to the skies, traveling up to 80 mi (around 130 km) per day.

Ready to roost

Reaching warmer roosting places is the aim of the entire journey as, being cold-blooded, the butterflies would struggle to survive the cold winters of northern areas. Imagos often select the same roosting trees chosen by previous generations, but no one knows how they do this. The Mexican forests prove to be the perfect environment for resting insects—cool enough for their metabolisms to slow down but not so cold as to freeze them.

◄ When butterflies roost they go into a form of suspended animation (a state of near inactivity), slowly utilizing their stores of body fat. Some may fall to the forest floor, others risk being eaten by birds.

► The monarchs' winter home was a mystery until some were tagged to monitor migrations and populations.

TAG@KU.EDU
MONARCH WATCH
1-888-TAGGING
GJE 148

Homeward bound

Spring warmth wakens the butterflies. They become more active, and start to feed and mate. They begin the journey northward, later joined by their offspring, who complete the final leg of the migration.

BEACH Party

Drawn by the light of the Moon, thousands of olive ridley turtles emerge from the sea and pour onto the shore. All turtle species come onto land to lay their eggs. But only ridley turtles lay simultaneously, in a spectacular ritual that dates back millions of years.

▼ Like all reptiles, turtles breathe air. They nest on land so that their embryos can breathe while they are developing inside the eggs.

▼ Females dig their nests at their own birthplace. They usually lay up to three clutches of eggs each year.

Arribada!

The Playa Ostional in Costa Rica hosts up to 20,000 visiting female olive ridley turtles most months. Known by the locals as the Arribada ("arrival from the sea"), this mass appearance is an example of a smart reproductive strategy that is common in the natural world. By laying their fertilized eggs simultaneously, the females are hoping there is safety in numbers—for themselves and their young.

Quick dig

Although they are swift-moving and agile in water, the female turtles are cumbersome on land. They haul their heavy bodies up the beach and dig a hole in the soft sand with their flipperlike forelimbs. It's hard work, and the turtles breathe loudly and deeply as they labor. The hind limbs scoop deeper to create an egg pit, and about 100 eggs are dropped into it. The mother covers her eggs with sand and, her job done, she heads back to the sea.

▼ Newly hatched turtles head for the sea. They will stay there for up to 15 years. Females remember the smell of their beach, and return to lay their own eggs.

Hatch and dash

Baby turtles develop inside their eggs for 45 to 60 days. The ambient temperature affects their development, with lower temperatures more likely to produce males than females. When they hatch, the turtles must make a dash for the sea, avoiding any predators that lurk nearby.

▼ Fewer than one in 100 eggs hatch and the tiny turtles, with their eyes barely open, sniff the breeze and run for the sea. The run helps develop their lungs.

▼ Up to 300 people are employed to collect and sort eggs from nests at Playa Ostional.

AT ONE POINT THERE WERE FEWER THAN SEVERAL HUNDRED KEMP'S RIDLEY TURTLES LEFT. CONSERVATION EFFORTS HAVE RESTORED THE POPULATION TO 1,000 NESTING FEMALES.

Egg harvest

Playa Ostional is the only place in the world where it is legal to harvest turtle eggs. Every year, the local community harvests about four million eggs for sale and consumption. Although the harvest is controlled and regarded as sustainable, neighboring communities appear to fare better economically by conserving their turtle nests and encouraging tourism instead.

NATURE'S Nomads

Herds of wildebeest trek through African grasslands in search of food and water. Their epic journey takes them across the Mara and Gremeti rivers, where crocodiles lie in wait. The clever crocs target weak animals at the edges of the herd, so one false step could prove fatal.

Crossing the river

The wildebeest travel in a continuous circle between the southern plains of the Serengeti and the more northerly lands of the Maasai Mara. Every year they walk for about 1,800 mi (2,900 km). These marathon migrations are punctuated by dangerous river crossings, where hordes of crocodiles gather in hungry expectation.

Safety in numbers

In an overwhelming breeding spectacle, 8,000 calves may be be born in one day of the wildebeest calving season, which typically lasts for a few weeks between January and March. Each female gives birth to a single calf, surrounded by other wildebeest for protection. The calves vastly outnumber the potential predators—a breeding strategy that gives the herd a reasonable chance of maintaining its population size.

Calves are usually born at the start of the rains, when conditions are most favorable. They are able to stand within 15 minutes of birth.

Quickfire crocs

Most crocodiles hunt alone. Nile crocodiles, however, have learned where wildebeest cross the rivers and adapted their behavior to enjoy a feeding bonanza. They work as a group, lining up at crossing points and waiting for the wildebeest to make a move. The crocodiles identify vulnerable individuals, block their route to the shore, and close in for the kill.

A wildebeest endeavors to escape the predator's jaws, but at up to 20 ft (6 m) in length, Nile crocodiles are forceful adversaries.

ROUND ROUTE
The wildebeest leave the north in the dry season, following the rains southward to calve. They return north via pastures in the west.

KENYA

Dry season

TANZANIA

Rainy season

Now you see me...
An estimated two million grazing animals are constantly on the move across the African grassland. Most of the migrating animals are wildebeest, but about 200,000 zebras form part of this enormous cavalcade, finding protection from lions by lurking within the wildebeest herd.

Zebras can only survive by constantly moving to new grazing areas. Hiding among vast wildebeest herds provides them with cover from predators.

White-bearded wildebeest are one of five subspecies of blue wildebeest. They migrate in search of food, water, and phosphorous, a mineral that the females need to produce milk.

SARDINE Run

Scores of frantically working tails whisk the water along South Africa's east coast into a seething mass. Witness the sardine run—one of nature's most incredible events. This multitude of fish is a major crowd-puller and predators flock to feast here in their thousands.

▶ Cape gannets dive for fish. If they overeat they may not be able to take flight again easily, and will themselves become tasty snacks for sharks.

Chasing currents

From May to July in most years, millions of sardines are driven by their reproductive instincts to head toward their spawning grounds. Their journey takes them northward along the eastern coast of South Africa, following cool winter water currents. Scientists have suggested that the more northerly waters provide a good environment for the sardine eggs and fry (newly hatched young) to survive— and undertaking this risky journey is a price worth paying for the better start in life it gives their young.

Feeding frenzy

Numerous predators swim alongside the school, gradually forcing the sardines close to the shore and trapping them. Marlins, tuna, seals, sharks, gannets, dolphins, and whales are just some of the hungry hunters that come to enjoy the feast.

ALBATROSSES, PENGUINS, AND ORCAS MAY TRAVEL THOUSANDS OF MILES FROM THE SOUTHERN OCEAN TO FEAST ON SARDINES.

Star attraction

The only defense the massive, shimmering schools have against the predators is to close ranks, creating "bait balls" to confuse them. A tightly packed swirling circle of silvery sardines distracts some animals, but the most tenacious predators are scarcely put off by this last-ditch attempt at survival. Tourists and fishermen are drawn to the spectacle, even wading into the water with nets to catch sardines—optimistic that the prowling sharks have their eyes firmly set on a fish dinner.

▼ Fishermen look for telltale signs of sardines, such as diving birds and pods of dolphins, and can land thousands of fish in one net.

▶ A sailfish uses its bill to jab at fish in the bait ball as it swims past before rushing back in to swallow them whole.

▲ Sharks are normally solitary animals but copper, dusky, bull, ragged-tooth, and tiger sharks all appear along the sardine run.

Follow that food

The mechanics of the sardine run largely remain a mystery. A drop in ocean temperature appears to trigger the headlong rush along the coast, which explains why the run sometimes fails to occur in exceptionally warm years. The fish follow cold currents that carry huge quantities of their food, plankton, and as they swim they congregate in enormous schools, each containing millions of fish, and stretching for many miles.

FLASH Mob!

F or centuries, human ancestors believed that some animal populations spontaneously arose from dust, soil, or even rotting flesh. They had witnessed the sudden, awesome appearance of thousands of animals, with no clues as to their origin.

Garter snakes swarm to generate heat and keep themselves warm. This helps them to mate more readily.

Best mates

With snow still lying on the ground, the first male red-sided garter snakes waken after a winter's hibernation. The spring warmth heralds the sudden appearance of tens of thousands more, forming seething masses that wait for the emergence of the first females. This surprising spectacle is the largest gathering of reptiles in the world. As each female wakens, she finds herself surrounded by up to 50 males in a tangled heap, ready and willing to mate.

▼ An enormous swarm of mayflies takes off from the water and frenetically turns its attention to mating.

One day

Hundreds of thousands of mayflies lurk in a pond, invisible until one special day. Surviving as nymphs hidden in the pond's sediment, the mayflies feed and grow to adulthood. A change in temperature is the most likely trigger that spurs the mayflies into action. They simultaneously change into adults with wings, and surface. In their adult form, mayflies do not even live long enough to feed—they mate and die within one to three days of emerging.

Big babies

When millions of periodical cicadas hatch at the same time, scientists call the phenomenon a "mass emergence." But to anyone nearby this astonishing event means just one thing: a relentless chorus of raucous mating calls. The bugs survive underground for 13 or 17 years (depending on the species) as nymphs, feeding on tree roots. When their internal alarm clocks go off, the adults dig their way out and prepare to mate. The males sing to attract females, but it is a short swan song: they survive in their adult form for just a few weeks.

Up to 1.5 million cicadas may emerge simultaneously in just one acre (4,000 sq m) of land to molt (shed their exoskeletons), mate, and die.

Spooky silk

When tent caterpillars seemingly appear from nowhere, they do it in style. Millions emerge from their tiny eggs simultaneously, smothering trees and bushes with their squirming bodies. The caterpillars surround themselves with a protective shield of silk. After gorging on leaves, they return to their tents to digest their food, untroubled by birds and other predators that are deterred by the sticky silk.

◀ Caterpillars of the ermine spindle moth swarm over a tree, stripping it of foliage and leaving a ghostly memento of their presence.

The RIVALS

Animals are driven by the need to reproduce, and this causes the males of some species to risk life and limb in an attempt to pass on their genes. Fierce competition for mates can lead to bloody battles, and breathtaking wildlife spectacles.

Fight on!

Smart animals give fair warning before launching into a fight. In elephant seals, loud roars, head shaking, and other displays of strength and size may be enough to win dominance without taking any physical risks. But if all else fails, male seals enter the ring with gusto. They rush headlong at one another and slap their heads and necks together, head-butting and biting with ferocity. Thick layers of fat and muscle around their heads and throats provide some protection, but the violent encounters usually result in injuries, and fatalities are common.

Round

1

Hercules beetle

Weapon of choice: Giant pincer horns
Damage: Can slash opponent in two

10 STRENGTH FACTOR

VS.

Hercules beetle

Regarded, for its size, as one of the strongest animals on Earth, the tropical Hercules beetle uses its pincerlike horns to grab hold of its opponent, lift it, and go for a body slam. This American mini-monster may be only 6 in (15 cm) long but it can lift 850 times its own weight. A victor wins mating rights with any female spectator.

Giraffe V Giraffe

5 STRENGTH FACTOR

Weapon of choice: Absurdly long neck
Damage: Rarely fatal

Adult male giraffes living in small groups frequently spar with one another, especially when fertile females are around. Known as necking, they fight by walloping their necks against each other and using their heads like clubs. A well-timed swing can knock an opponent to the ground, leaving it temporarily unconscious.

◄ When male elephant seals fight, they inflate their noses and roar. Their roars are so loud they can be heard from miles away.

SPANISH IBEX

8 STRENGTH FACTOR

SPANISH IBEX

Weapon of choice: Huge horns
Damage: Serious flesh wounds may lead to death

Dueling is common in horned animals, but male Spanish ibex are gladiators without equal. Males battle for mating rights, relying on their toughened skulls and muscle-packed shoulders for defense during fights, known as "ruts." Despite this protection, horns that grow to 26 in (75 cm) in length can deliver deadly wounds.

SO MACHO

In the animal world, it is not uncommon for males to try to mate with as many females as possible. To do so they may have to fight off other males, and in these instances great strength, size, and weapons are an advantage. As a result, the males of some species grow to be enormous compared to females, and often labor under impressive horns or antlers, have immensely muscular shoulders, or possess outsize fangs and claws.

A male elephant seal can weigh four or five times as much as a female.

Think PINK

Shocking pink flamingos flock to Africa's soda lakes, strutting and gliding across the rich waters. More than one m ÕlŠn lesser flamingos arrive to feed and dance, and create what is regarded as one of the world's most beautiful sights.

Soda soup

A number of soda lakes line the Great Rift Valley in Africa. The blistering heat and a high concentration of alkaline minerals in the water have created basins of caustic soda that are hostile to most forms of life. However, tiny life forms called cyanobacteria can thrive here. The population of one type, *Spirulina*, periodically explodes and turns the water to a thick, nutritious, pea-green "soup." It is favored by flamingos, which gather in large numbers to feast on a bumper crop.

▶ Tens of thousands of flamingos can descend on Kenya's Lake Bogoria at a time.

Dazzling dancers

Millions of pink flamingos arrive at a soda lake to prepare for their extraordinary courtship dances. They begin by flicking their heads and flapping their wings, but soon move into a synchronized parade. Groups of marching flamingos meld into larger congregations that move so smoothly through the water that they appear to be gliding or skating. Eventually—no one knows how—pair bonds begin to form and nesting soon follows.

Flame birds

Flamingos are named from the Latin word *flamma*, or flame. Their extraordinary color comes from *Spirulina*, which contain carotenoid pigments. The flamingos eat the cyanobacteria and the pigments are transferred to their feathers. To feed, flamingos use their large feet to stir the water, bringing the *Spirulina* to the surface. Then they swing their heads, upside down, from side to side. Inside their mouths are thousands of thin plates that strain the tiny organisms from the water.

▼ Even while feeding, flamingos are able to keep a watchful eye open for predators.

◀ During their courtship dances, groups of male flamingos break up, reunite, and change direction simultaneously.

DANGER AHEAD!
Africa's lesser flamingos are declining in number because their soda lake ecosystems are threatened. Commercial extraction of soda ash from the lakes damages the habitat, but growing populations of people around the lakes are also having a significant impact. More water is being drawn from the rivers that feed the lakes for agricultural use, and pollution entering the lakes is on the rise.

▲ Hyenas run alongside the lake, hoping to get lucky and grab a bird as it takes off.

SWARM!

A single swarm of 20 million bats may seem a frightening prospect, but these small flying mammals are helpful, not harmful. Mexican free-tailed bats form some of the greatest congregations of animals on Earth, and tens of millions may inhabit just one cave. These colonies need an enormous quantity of food to survive, and their diet is made up entirely of insects, many of which are agricultural pests.

NIGHT FRIGHT

THE FLAPPING HORDES LEAVE THEIR ROOST TO HUNT

Invasion of the KILLER BEES

To the untrained eye, an Africanized or "killer" bee looks just like a European honeybee. Killer bees, however, are very aggressive, and quick to swarm when food is scarce, or when they want to create new nests. Swarms can detect people 50 ft (15 m) away from their nests and don't hesitate to sting in defense. They move swiftly to attack, and will even chase people some distance. While one sting is rarely fatal, hundreds of stings can prove to be lethal.

THE ACTIONS OF A SINGLE BEE, BIRD, BAT, OR BUG MAY APPEAR INSIGNIFICANT, BUT WHEN SPECIES BAND TOGETHER THEY CAN PUNCH FAR ABOVE THEIR WEIGHT AND HAVE A DRAMATIC IMPACT. THE MOST AWESOME SWARMS NUMBER MILLIONS OF INDIVIDUALS, AND MAKE FOR A SPECTACULAR SIGHT.

A TAWNY MASS HOVERS AND SWIRLS OVER THE AFRICAN SCRUBLAND...

PHENOMENAL FLOCKS

From a distance it could be mistaken for a fast-moving dust cloud, but a closer look reveals that it is actually a congregation of the world's most abundant bird—the red-billed quelea.

Thousands of these weaver birds flock to feast on seed crops and trees, stripping them bare. There are more than 1.5 billion red-billed queleas in total, and some flocks are so huge they can take five hours to pass overhead.

A SWARM OF LOCUSTS MAY NUMBER 16,000,000,000 INDIVIDUALS!

LOCUST PLAGUE!

WHEN THE POPULATION OF LOCUSTS IN AN AREA OUTGROWS THE AVAILABLE FOOD, IT'S TIME TO SWARM. . .

- A locust eats its bodyweight in food every day.
- A swarm can devour 35,000 tons of food in 24 hours.
- In 2004, around 69 billion locusts gathered in a mega-swarm, devastating parts of northwest Africa.
- A swarm can travel 80 mi (around 130 km) or more in one day.
- One long-distance migration in 1988 saw locusts travel from West Africa to the Caribbean—that's about 3,000 mi (nearly 5,000 km) in ten days.

▶ In 2004, Senegal suffered one of the world's worst locust invasions.

Marine
Marvels

Some of nature's most awesome events occur beneath the surface of the sea and at its coasts. Hidden from human eyes, convoys of lobsters march across the seabed, while blooms of golden jellyfish gently propel themselves through salty waters, and colorful squid dance for their mates.

Golden jellies

Up to ten mōlŝn golden jellyfish migrate in the marine lakes at Palau, in the Pacific Ocean. The saline lakes are enclosed, but stŌl experience tidal flows because ocean water has access to them. Every morning, the jellyfish move up to the surface of the water and swim across the lake, following the course of the Sun. Sunlight is essential for the health of the algae that live inside the jellyfish and provide them with energy.

Flash dance

The Australian giant cuttlefish grows to 5 ft (1.5 m) in length. In winter, many thousands migrate to shallow waters where the males dazzle females with spectacular displays of color. The dances begin with a show of size, as the males stretch out their "arms" to prove their superiority, and zebra patterns whizz down their flanks. Like other cuttlefish, these giants can change color in an instant, and they produce a show so impressive that divers, as well as female cuttlefish, gather to enjoy the performance.

▼ A male broadclub cuttlefish shields his mate from a potential rival during their courtship ritual.

Quick march

Late summer storms spur Caribbean spiny lobsters into action. As their coastal waters cool, and low winds make the shallow waters murky, the lobsters get ready to move. Lined up in single file, the intrepid crustaceans march to deeper areas, where warm water speeds the development of the females' eggs. They will mate here, and return to the shallows in spring.

▲ Each spiny lobster touches the tail fan of the lobster in front as it walks, forming an orderly line. It's a bizarre event, and one which few people ever witness.

▼ Golden jellyfish bask in sunlight so that the microscopic algae that live inside them have access to the light rays they need to survive.

Land ahoy!

When a killer whale approaches an ice floe or land, there is little warning other than the sudden appearance of its black dorsal fin. Also known as orcas, these super predators come in search of a meaty seal takeaway. Using enormous strength and speed, orcas fling themselves onto shore to grab their prey. When a seal is resting on ice floes, an orca can tip the frozen slab, so lunch almost rolls into its mouth!

▶ An orca, despite its huge bulk, heaves itself onto shore, surprising a sea lion that has no time to escape.

SPINY LOBSTERS MIGRATE UP TO 30 MI (ABOUT 50 KM) IN A FEW DAYS. BY WALKING IN SINGLE FILE THEY REDUCE DRAG, SO THEY CAN MARCH AT DOUBLE-QUICK TIME!

NONSTOP Godwits

Many birds undertake phenomenal journeys during their seasonal migrations, but bar-tailed godwits are the most awesome of all aviators. They embark on epic nonstop journeys that take them halfway round the world.

Globetrotters

Godwits are wading birds, with an unremarkable appearance that belies their incredible stamina. They reside in the cool tundra regions of the north, where they nest and raise their chicks in summer. The birds then move southward to feed and stock up their body fat until it constitutes more than half of their bodyweight. They can then fly nonstop southward, crossing the Equator to reach feeding grounds.

Extreme endurance

Godwits migrating south never rest, eat, or drink, even though some of them are just two months old. As winter approaches in the Southern Hemisphere, the birds prepare for the return journey. Some of them may stop off in Europe en route, to enjoy milder weather than that endured by the birds that make it back to the tundra.

▶ This muscular male godwit is leaving Norway. His ultimate destination will be Australia, New Zealand, or South Africa.

The record-setter

A female godwit known as E7 was tracked undertaking the longest, fastest nonstop migratory flight in the world. After leaving New Zealand in March 2007, E7 stopped in China to rest and feed. She then flew onward to Alaska, where she raised two chicks. On August 29, E7 left for her nonstop journey back to New Zealand, and reached her feeding grounds in just eight days.

Alaska (U.S.)

1–15 May

4,500 mi (7,237 km)

CHINA

PACIFIC OCEAN

29 Aug – 7 Sept

7,200 mi (11,570 km)

6,340 mi (10,219 km)

17–24 March

Start/ Finish

NEW ZEALAND

RED KNOT PIT STOP

Red knots achieve a similar long distance feat to bar-tailed godwits, migrating between the southerly parts of South America and the Canadian Arctic. Each journey covers about 10,000 mi (17,000 km). They make pit stops on the way to feed and rest, but the most spectacular of these coincides with the mass arrival of horseshoe crabs at Delaware Bay in North America. The arthropods congregate to mate, and their eggs are perfect packets of protein and energy.

▲ Hordes of hungry birds, including red knots, descend on Delaware Bay, and spend several weeks gorging on horseshoe crab eggs.

SEA SWALLOWS

Arctic terns don't care that the shortest distance between two points is a straight line. Their remarkable migration between the Poles follows a figure-of-eight pattern that adds several thousand miles to their journey. The detour makes sense, because it allows the terns to save energy by traveling on the prevailing wind. Every year, a tern may fly 43,000 mi (70,000 km).

▼ Arctic terns are sometimes known as sea swallows, because of their aerobatic skills, and stamina in the sky.

ARCTIC TERNS CAN LIVE FOR UP TO 20 YEARS. ONE BIRD MAY FLY MORE THAN 200,000 MI (322,000 KM) IN ITS LIFE—THAT'S EQUIVALENT TO FLYING FROM EARTH TO THE MOON.

BLOOMING Brilliant

Plants operate on a different timescale to animals and most reproduce, feed, and breathe without making any obvious movements or undergoing large changes. So when awesome events happen, they are especially momentous.

▲ As a titan arum flower grows it emits a nauseating smell. Its top tip eventually reaches a height of up to 10 ft (3 m) above the ground.

Sudden stench

The flowering of the stinky titan arum is unpredictable but when it happens, the event is spectacular. The tropical plant produces a massive flowering structure (called an inflorescence) from a tuber that weighs 150 lb (70 kg) or more—it's the largest tuber in the plant kingdom.

The thick, leathery Rafflesia petals unfurl overnight, into a flower that measures up to 42 in (107 cm) across.

Corpse flower

The Rafflesia is said to smell of rotting flesh, but it is better known for its looks—it grows unobtrusively before erupting into the world's largest flower. However the blooming is unpredictable, and each flower lasts only a few days. Rafflesia grows as a parasite on rain forest vines and relies on small flies to pollinate its flower.

Fig feast

When a giant fig tree produces its fruit, there are rich pickings for everyone. Since these trees only fruit once every two years, the inhabitants of its Indonesian rain forest home turn up in their droves to eat their fill, including long-tailed macaques, red leaf monkeys, orangutans, gibbons, and thousands of birds. For a short while the tree becomes the hub of a noisy feasting crowd, and after a few weeks the bonanza is over.

◀ A gray gibbon swings between the branches of a fig tree to dine on its juicy fruits.

BAMBOO SHOOTS CAN GROW MORE THAN 12 IN (AROUND 30 CM) IN A SINGLE DAY, AND MAY REACH 100 FT (ABOUT 30 M) IN A SINGLE GROWING SEASON.

Burst into bloom

Bamboo forests are formed from tall-growing grasses, and once every 30 to 40 years a unique phenomenon, not yet understood by scientists, sweeps through them. It is a process called masting, when all the bamboo plants of one species spontaneously burst into flower over a large area. All the plants then simultaneously die.

▼ Giant pandas feed on bamboo. They feast during a masting event, but then face starvation when an entire bamboo forest dies afterward.

▲ Flies are trapped, turned into a tasty soup by digestive juices, and then absorbed by the plant.

Meat eater

Hidden in the boggy undergrowth in North or South Carolina, U.S., the Venus flytrap is easy to overlook. But a keen eye and great patience can be greatly rewarding: these plants are killers. Unlike most plants they do not make their food—they eat it. Their sensitive leaves form traps, and when a fly crawls inside, they respond by snapping shut—as fast as the blink of an eye.

The natural world is a dangerous place, where death may be just around the corner. When a predator goes in for a perfectly timed attack on its prey, the task of grabbing a meal becomes a dazzling natural spectacle.

Stoop and scoop

The moment when a peregrine falcon turns a hover into a stoop (power-dive) is so sudden that catching sight of it is a rare privilege for any wildlife watcher. These raptors are the fastest animals in the world, but they owe their hunting prowess as much to the accuracy of their eyesight as to their speed. A stoop brings the predator toward its aerial target at estimated speeds of over 200 mph (about 320 km/h).

TOP SECRET

▼ With forward-facing eyes, a peregrine can focus on its prey even while in a vertical dive.

Squeeze me

Some snakes take their time over lunch, and are prepared to wait weeks between meals. When the opportunity to feed arises, however, constrictor snakes are swift to strike. Once a python or boa has gripped the prey in its jaws, it wraps its huge, muscular coils around the body and slowly squeezes. This death grip forces all the air from the prey's lungs until it suffocates.

▲ A rock python can open its jaws wide enough to engulf the body of a ground squirrel.

Going in for the kill

Solitary big cats rely on stealth, speed, and strength to kill. Yet while they are supreme predators, their prey has also evolved ways to stay alive, relying on alertness, speed, and a dogged determination to survive. As many as three out of four cheetah hunts are unsuccessful, and some tigers fail to make a kill 90 percent of the time they pursue prey.

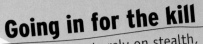

▶ A cheetah keeps its prey in its sights as it stalks to within sprinting distance.

Pack attack

Like many hunters, wolves often hunt under the cover of dark. Their natural forest habitats provide extra cover, and help these carnivores to remain hidden from even the most alert prey. Wolves usually hunt as packs of up to eight family members, and a successful hunt requires great coordination between all individuals.

▲ The alpha (dominant) pair of wolves feed first. The other pack members are only allowed to join in when the appetites of the alpha pair are sated.

Tongue tricksters

A chameleon's lightning-quick attack is so speedy that it is almost impossible to catch with the naked eye. The reptile's super-sticky tongue catapults out of its mouth at 13.4 mph (21.6 km/h), and accelerates from 0 to 20 ft (0 to 6 m) in 20 milliseconds. Even flies, which have lightning-quick reactions, are too slow to escape.

▶ The tip of a Madagascan parson's chameleon's tongue works like a small suction cup.

ONE YEAR

January

Many hundreds of bald eagles gather at their winter habitat at Klamath Basin marshes in Oregon, U.S. These majestic birds spend the coldest months of the year on the frozen water, feeding on waterfowl.

Every minute of every day, extraordinary events occur in the natural world. Driven by the instinct to survive, there is always an awesome spectacle to be seen somewhere. Follow a selection of nature's highlights around the globe and be amazed from January to December.

May

A four-hour trek through drizzle and high vegetation in the Rwandan cloud forest may be rewarded with the sight of a family of endangered mountain gorillas. Some have become accustomed to human presence, and will continue to play and eat while spectators watch.

April

Two million migratory birds gather around Broome in Western Australia to begin their 6,000 mi (10,000 km) flight to the Northern Hemisphere, along the Australasian flyway—one of the world's greatest migratory flight paths.

August

The Danum Valley in Borneo is hard to reach, but the trip deep into a rain forest is worthwhile. Watch orangutans in the wild while you can—they face extinction within 20 years because their habitat is being replaced by palm oil plantations.

September

Wish You Were Here!

Male elks in Yellowstone National Park, Wyoming, U.S., begin the rutting season. Furious fighting precedes mating.

October

February

Whale sightings are at their best in the Southern Hemisphere's summer. Minke, humpback (left), beaked, fin, southern right, and blue whales can be spotted around the Antarctic Peninsula and into the Southern Ocean. They come to feast, making the most of a temporary abundance of food.

March

Tigers are one of the world's most elusive big cats, and this is a good time to see them in the Sunderban and Ranthambore Tiger Reserves in India.

June

Sloth bears in Sri Lanka are normally nocturnal, but in June they become active in the day as well, so they can feast on the trees' ripening fruit.

July

The glorious purple emperor butterfly is an elusive woodland inhabitant. This is the best time to see it flying around the U.K.'s native oak trees.

Only the males have the resplendent purple sheen, which is created when light is refracted by the wing scales. Females are brown.

November

On clear mornings by the upper Tambopata River in Peru, hundreds of macaws arrive to lick clay from the bank. Eating earth is called "geophagy," and it occurs in several animal species. The clay contains minerals that may be useful supplements to an animal's diet.

Thousands of polar bears gather at Churchill, Manitoba in Canada. They are waiting for the Hudson River to freeze over so they can hunt.

December

In Japan, China, and Russia, Japanese red-crowned cranes gather to begin their beautiful, synchronized courtship dances.

On the HOOF

Pronghorns and caribou undertake the longest migrations of any land animals in the New World. Long ago, there may have been millions of these deer trekking across the North American plains, but interference from humans has added many obstacles to their journeys.

Going the distance

Caribou herds may number thousands, and make 3,000-mi (about 5,000-km) journeys through the course of a single year as they move to find better grazing areas, to calve, and to avoid the winter's worst weather and the summer's biting insects. Caribou can be flexible in their routes, so one year's migration might differ in route and distance from the previous year's, and may involve crossing water as well as land. Caribou can swim very well, and their winter coats have hollow hairs, which help the deer to float high in the water.

Following the food

Further north, vast herds of caribou conduct their migrations with much less interference from people. Also known as reindeer, these hoofed mammals trek through the Arctic tundra and boreal regions, where food and humans are scarce, although caribou territories once extended much further south.

▶ Caribou from the Porcupine Herd forge onward in Alaska. Their progress is tracked by satellite so that scientists can document their migratory patterns.

▼ Bison are now being allowed to exercise their migration instincts. Until recently they were confined to national parks, such as Yellowstone in Wyoming, U.S.

Buffalo woes

Yellowstone National Park, in Wyoming, U.S., is home to one of the largest free-roaming herds of bison (also known as "buffalo"). They are direct descendants of the 30 million bison that once populated the Great Plains, before relentless hunting saw their numbers fall to just 1,091 in 1889. Efforts to conserve bison often fail when the animals' instinct to migrate puts them into conflict with farmers.

Many caribou migration routes require the herds to cross sizeable rivers.

Obstacle course

There are about half a million pronghorns in Wyoming, U.S.—about the same as the number of people. But almost 80 percent of the animals' ancient routes between winter feeding and summer calving grounds have disappeared beneath commercial developments. Now only one herd makes the seasonal journey, and the 100-mi (160-km) route tests the pronghorns' endurance to the limit. The natural landscape has been broken up by urbanization and roads to such an extent that reaching the calving ground is now an unnaturally hazardous exercise.

▼ Pronghorns cross busy roads and squeeze through barbed wire fences to reach their summer home.

ELEPHANTS
on the March

Elephants walk with intent when they are on the move. Driven by the need for water and food, a herd on the march creates a majestic procession that seems to operate with a single mind. These extremely intelligent animals are highly social and have strong family bonds.

ELEPHANTS CAN COMMUNICATE WITH EACH OTHER BY MAKING LOW-FREQUENCY RUMBLES. THE SOUNDS PASS THROUGH THE GROUND TO HERD MEMBERS, WHICH HEAR THE RUMBLES THROUGH THEIR FEET.

BIG APPETITES

An adult elephant needs to eat 350 lb (160 kg) of food every day, and may tear down branches to get fruit, strip bark, and even fell whole trees to feed. When a herd of these huge animals is confined to a small area it can inadvertently demolish its own food source, which is why elephants need massive territories, and many of them migrate to survive.

▼ As the length and severity of droughts in parts of Africa increase, herds of desert elephants spend their days wandering in search of water.

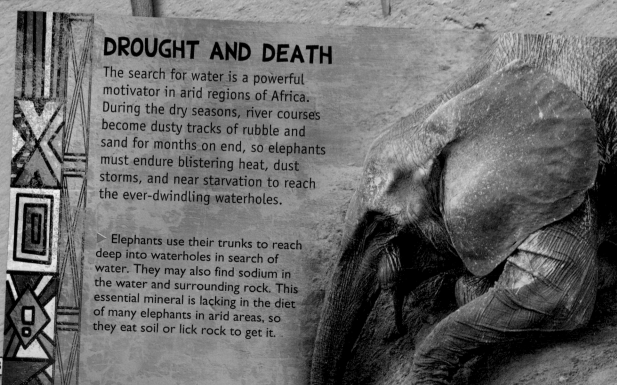

DROUGHT AND DEATH

The search for water is a powerful motivator in arid regions of Africa. During the dry seasons, river courses become dusty tracks of rubble and sand for months on end, so elephants must endure blistering heat, dust storms, and near starvation to reach the ever-dwindling waterholes.

▶ Elephants use their trunks to reach deep into waterholes in search of water. They may also find sodium in the water and surrounding rock. This essential mineral is lacking in the diet of many elephants in arid areas, so they eat soil or lick rock to get it.

▼ Elephants follow safe routes between waterholes and neighboring national parks and tourists congregate to view the spectacle.

ON THE RIGHT ROAD

The future is looking good for Namibia's migrating elephants—the largest elephant population in Africa. Since the value of the herds to the ecosystem and tourism has been appraised, conservation has been put high on the national agenda. Corridors—the pathways followed by migrating elephants—are now protected. Elephants in different areas face different problems, so conservation efforts have to be tailor-made to fit each region.

TEMPERATURES SOAR TO 120°F (49°C) IN MALI'S SAHEL REGION, WHILE ELEPHANTS COMPLETE ROUND TRIPS OF 300 MI (480 KM) EVERY YEAR TO FIND WATER AND FOOD.

▼ Up to ten African elephants descend on this Zambian lodge every October when the mango trees fruit. The hotel now encourages guests to enjoy the spectacle.

ELEPHANT IN THE ROOM

When hotels are built on ancient elephant corridors, the animals do not always understand that they should take a detour. A herd of elephants was not deterred by the erection of Mfuwe Lodge at South Luangwa National Park in Zambia—they simply walked right through the hotel's reception to reach the fruiting mango trees they have been visiting for generations.

INDEX

◀ Found in Asia, pit vipers have small, thick bodies and prehensile tails. They are typically green in color and feed on small animals, such as amphibians and birds.

INDEX

Entries in **bold** refer to main subject entries; entries in *italics* refer to illustrations.

ACKNOWLEDGMENTS

The publishers would like to thank the following sources for the use of their photographs:

KEY
A/AL=Alamy, B=Bridgeman, CO=Corbis, D=Dreamstime, F=Fotolia, FLPA=Frank Lane Picture Agency, GI=Getty Images, GW=Glow Images, IS=istockphoto.com, MP=Minden Pictures, N=Newscom, NG=National Geographic Creative, NPL=Nature Picture Library, P=Photoshot, PL=Photolibrary, R=Reuters, RF=Rex Features, S=Shutterstock, SJC=Stuart Jackson-Carter, SPL=Science Photo Library, SS=Superstock, TF=Topfoto

t=top, a=above, b=bottom/below, c=center, l=left, r=right, f=far, m=main, bg=background

COVER Steven Kazlowski/NPL, BACK COVER Michael Rosskothen/S, S, Dmitri Gomon/S, Jerry Bouwmeester/S, MarkMirror/S, PRELIMS 1 Volodymyr Goinyk/S, 2 Eric Isselee/S, 3 Catmando/S, Mogens Trolle/S, 4 S, Galyna Andrushko/S

PREHISTORIC GIANTS 6–7 WALTER MYERS/SPL, 8 SJC, 9 SJC, 8–9 Sergey Mikhaylov/S, 8–9(bg) EcOasis/S, 8(br) Reinhard Dirscherl/FLPA, 8(cl) Jaime Chirinos/SPL, 8(sketches) pavila/S, 9(bc) KUCO/S, 11 The Natural History Museum/A, 11 My Good Images/S, 10–11 SJC, 10–11(bg) Reinhold Leitner/S, 10, 11(labels) Mrsiraphol/S, 10(diagrams) grynold/S, 10(scale) Jakkrit Orrasri/S, 10(t) happydancing/S, 10(tags) val lawless/S, 10(tl border) colors/S, 10(tl) RICHARD BIZLEY/SPL, 11(cr) nuttakit/S, 11(tc) De Agostini/GI, 12–13(b) geographlo/S, 12(bl) Sabena Jane Blackbird/A, 12(main) JAIME CHIRINOS/SPL, 12(tl) Roman Sigaev/S, 13(br) CHRISTIAN DARKIN/SPL, 13(t) JAIME CHIRINOS/SPL, 12–13(main) Sergey Skleznev/A, 12(cl) Topfoto.co.uk, 13(bc) Johan Swanepoel/S, 13(tr) JAIME CHIRINOS/SPL, 16 Kostyantyn Ivanyshen/S, 14–15 LEONELLO CALVETTI/SPL, 14(l) ROGER HARRIS/SPL, 16–17(c bg) Lokichen/S, 16–17(t) Magnia/S, 16, 17(bl) matyas/S, 18 (c) Michael Rosskothen/S, 18(bl) DEA PICTURE LIBRARY/UIG/RF, 19(c) Stocktrek Images, Inc/A, 19(br) Stocktrek Images, Inc/A, 19(t) dpa picture alliance/A, 18 SJC, 20(b) Stocktrek Images, Inc/A, 20(c bg) Bojan Dzodan/S, 20(main bg) fotomak/S, 21(b) Stocktrek Images, Inc/A, 21(cr) Georgios Kollidas/S, 21(t) NHPA/P, 22(c) Catmando/S, 22(r) JULIUS T CSOTONYI/SPL, 22(l) Stocktrek Images, Inc/A, 22(main) Stefano Paterna/A, 23(bl) Stocktrek Images, Inc/A, 23(tr) MEHAU KULYK/SPL, 22–3 val lawless/S, 22–3(bg) macknimal/S, 22–3(string) sniegirova mariia/S, 24–5(bc) Olga Selyutina/S, 24(bl) Stocktrek Images, Inc/A, 24(cr) Q-Images/A, 24(tl) Kevin Schafer/CO, 24(tr) JOSE ANTONIO PEÑAS/SPL, 25(c) GI, 25(bl) CHRIS HELLIER/SPL, 25(cl) nuttakit/S, 25(cr) De Agostini Picture Library/P, 25(horn) PASCAL GOETGHELUCK/SPL, 25(tl) BW Folsom/S, 25(tr) MARK GARLICK/SPL, 26–7(main) Pavel L Photo and Video/S, 26(bc) JAIME CHIRINOS/SPL, 26(cr) JAIME CHIRINOS/SPL, 26(feathers) Potapov Alexander/S, 26(man) Tsomka/S, 26(tr) JAIME CHIRINOS/SPL,

26(woman) Layland Masuda/S, 27(c) JAIME CHIRINOS/SPL, 27(br) National Geographic/GI, 27(girl) yykkaa/S, 28–9 Ron and Joe/S, 28–9(drawings) lavitrei/S, 28(bl) JAIME CHIRINOS/SPL, 28(c/bg) Irina Solatges/S, 28(c/bg) Irina Solatges/S, 28(circle bg) dedoma/S, 28(tr) Florilegius/A, 28(wall bg) Bruce Amos/S, 29(border) rickwade/S, 29(br) JAIME CHIRINOS/SPL, 29(tr) National Geographic Image Collection/A, 30–1(bg) Tomaz Kunst/S, 30(b) SCOTTCHAN/S, 30(bl) bikeriderlondon/S, 30(main) Galyna Andrushko/S, 30(panel) S, 30(paper) Picsfive/S, 30(t) Inna G/S, 31(br main) AF archive/A, 31(br panel) Lukiyanova Natalia/frenta/S, 32 SJC, 33 SJC, 32–3(main) JAIME CHIRINOS/SPL, 32(cl) Timur Kulgarin/S, 33(bl) DK Limited/CO, 34(c) Ryan M. Bolton/S, 34–5(main bg) s oleg/S, 34–5(objects) moleskin/S, 34, 35(labels) kikka8835/S, 34(bc) DK Limited/C, 34(br) Daniel Eskridge/Stocktrek Images/CO, 34(cl) Nicku/S, 34(cl) My Good Images/S, 34(map) mattalia/S, 34(t main) Hein Nouwens/S, 34(t/bg) Leigh Prather/S, 35(b/main) JAIME CHIRINOS/SPL, 35(bc) Ryan M. Bolton/S, 35(tl) Andrew Rubtsov/A, 35(tr fossil) DK Limited/CO, 35(tr main) JAIME CHIRINOS/SPL, 35(watch) Bombaert Patrick/S, 36–7(b) Kamenetskiy Konstantin/S, 36–7(br) Apples Eyes Studio/S, 36–7(main) Ted Horowitz/CO, 36(br) NATURAL HISTORY MUSEUM, LONDON/SPL, 36(l) Jarek Janosek/S, 37(rb) Walter Myers /Stocktrek Images/CO, 37(rc) MAURICIO ANTON/SPL, 37(rt) North Wind Picture Archives/A, 37(tr) DNY/iStockphoto.com, 38 SJC, 39 SJC, 38(cl/bg) Miloje/S, 38–9(bg) Loskutnikov/S, 38(metal) Andrey Kuzmin/S, 40–1(c) Stocktrek Images, Inc/A, 40–1(bc) Phil Degginger/A, 40(bc) Vixit/S, 40(bl) PHILIPPE PLAILLY/SPL, 40(tags) kikka8869/S, 41(c) Robert Landau/CO, 41(br frame) Mikhail hoboton Popov/S, 41(tr) KIYOSHI OTA/epa/CO, 41(cl) Hans Winke/A

AWESOME ANIMALS 42–3 Christian Ziegler/MP/FLPA 44(t) Jurgen & Christine Sohns/FLPA, (b) Hugh Lansdown/FLPA 45(t) Stephen Dalton/NPL, (c) Stephen Dalton/NHPA, (b) Gisela Delpho/P 46(m) Jurgen & Christine Sohns/FLPA, (bl) Kim Taylor/NPL 47(t) Stephen Dalton/NPL, (b) Hue Chee Kong/S 48–9(bg) Alex Kuzovlev, (m) Reinhard Dirscherl/P 48(t) Natutik/S 49(t) Michael & Patricia Fogden/MP/FLPA, (br) Malcolm Schuyl/FLPA 50–1(bg) S, (bullet holes) Krisdog/D, (nails) dusan964/S, (wanted posters) Chyrko Olena/S, (keys) Simon Bratt/S 50(tl) Konstantin Sutyagin/S, (tr) Fred Bavendam/MP/FLPA, (bl) Frank Stober/Imagebroker/FLPA, (br) ZSSD/MP/FLPA, (br, bg) Kirsty Pargeter/F 51(tl) Austin J Stevens/P, (tr) Norbert Wu/MP/FLPA, (bl) Mitsuaki Iwago/MP/FLPA, (bl, bg) Triff/S, (br, handcuffs) Zsolt Horvath/S, (br, badge) Peter Polak/S 52–3(m) Piotr Naskrecki/MP/FLPA, (frame) Undergroundarts.co.uk/S 52(l) Piotr Naskrecki/MP/FLPA, (b) Mark Payne-Gill/NPL, (b, frame) Robert Adrian Hillman/S 53(t) S & D & K Maslowski/FLPA, (b) Ron Austing/FLPA 54–5(bg) Gudrun Muenz/S, (labels) Picsfive/S, (balloons) Michael C. Gray/S, (streamers) hans.slegers 54(tl) Ariadne Van Zandbergen/FLPA, (cl) Milena_/S, (c) Manfred Kage/P, (c, frame) Natalie-art/S, (br) Sherjaca/Shutterstock 55(tl) Eduardo Rivero/S, (tl, frame) vector-RGB/S,

106(tr) Michael & Patricia Fogden/Minden Pictures/FLPA, 107(b) LYNN M. STONE/NPL, 107(tl) Martin Zwick/NHPA/P, 107(tr) JONATHAN PLEDGER/S, 108–9(bg) Mrgreen/D, 108(bl) Doug Perrine/GI, 108(bl) Joe Gough/S, 108(bl) Oksana Nikolaieva/S, 108(bl) Alex Staroseltsev/S, 108(br) Winfried Wisniewski/GI, 108(br) Givaga/S, 108(cl) ivn3da/S, 108(cl) Nomad_Soul/S, 108(t) Jaimie Duplass/S, 108(tl) Nixx Photography/S, 108(tr) Anna Henly/GI, 108(tr) Kitch Bain/S, 108(tr) Oksana Nikolaieva/S, 108(tr) Miro art studio/S, 109(bc) Vitaly Raduntsev/S, 109(bl) Lyutskevych Dar'ya/S, 109(bl) Minden Pictures/SS, 109(cl) LHF Graphics/S, 109(cr) Julio Aldana/S, 109(cr) Nelia Sapronova/S, 109(t) Steven Kazlowski/Science Faction/CO, 109(t) discpicture/S, 110–11 Tischenko Irina/S, 110(br) Suzi Eszterhas/Minden Pictures/CO, 110(cl) Paul Souders/CO, 111(bc) Maridav/S, 111(br) Kathryn Jeffs/NPL, 111(cl) Doug Allan/NPL, 111(tr) Doug Allan/NPL, 112–13 moenez/S, 112–13 S, 112–13(bg) evv/S, 112(br) Loek Gerris/Foto Natura/Minden Pictures/CO, 112(br) Milkovasa/S, 112(br) Elliotte Rusty Harold/S, 112(cr) imagebroker/A, 112(cr) tonyz94/S, 112(tl) ra2studio/S, 113(bl) cynoclub/S, 113(bl) age fotostock/SS, 113(c) Potapov Alexander/S, 113(cl) Handout/Reuters/CO, 113(tl) David & Debi Henshaw/A, 113(tl) Sphinx Wang/S

AMAZING NATURE 114–15 Roman Golubenko/Solent/RF; 116–17 Wild Arctic Pictures/S; 116(bl) Joel Blit/S, (br) Robert Neumann/S, (cr) Sunset/FLPA, (l) Sunset/FLPA, (l) Jan Martin Will/S, (t) Slavolijub Pantelic/S; 117(br) Frans Lanting/FLPA, (cl) Rob Reijnen/Minden Pictures/FLPA, (t) Doug Allan/GI, (t) HABRDA/S, (t) Ton Lammerts/S; 118–19 Matthias Breiter/Minden Pictures/FLPA; 118(bl) beboy/S, (bl) Darren J. Bradley/S, (tl) Picsfive/S; 119(br) Sergey Gorshkov/Minden Pictures/FLPA, (l) GI, (r) Yva Momatiuk & John Eastcott/Minden Pictures/FLPA, (tl) Sergey Gorshkov/Minden Pictures/FLPA, (tl) Lukiyanova Natalia/frenta/S; 120–1 Ingo Arndt/Minden Pictures/FLPA, Ambient Ideas/S, Ingo Arndt/Minden Pictures/FLPA; 120(b) Cathy Keifer/IS, (b) Laurie Barr/S, (b) jaimaa/S, (b) Cathy Keifer/S, (cl) robertlamphoto/S, (cl) Sari Oneal/S, (l) HeinSchlebusch/S, (tl) Rtimages/S, (tl) Viktorya07/S; 121(br) Ingo Arndt/Minden Pictures/FLPA, (c) Tom Freeze/S, (cr) Le Do/S; 122–3 Konrad Wothe/GI, SVLuma/S; 122(bl) Solvin Zankl/NPL, (br) Marcel Jancovic/S, (c) Suzanna/S, (cr) Jerry Zitterman/S, (tl) Doug Perrine/NPL; 123(br) Jeffrey Rotman/CO, (br) Ben Jeayes/S, (br) Ruslan Nabiyev/S, (cl) Hallgerd/S, (cl) Benjamin Albiach Galan/S, (tl) Matthew W Keefe/S, (tr) Visuals Unlimited, Inc./Solvin Zankl/GI, (tr) Teeratas/S; 124–5(t) Andy Rouse/NPL; 124(bl) Paul McKenzie/GI, (cr) FLPA, (tl) SCOTTCHAN/S, (tl) irink/S; 125(b) Anup Shah/NPL, (bl) Iwona Grodzka/S, (tl) Zhukov Oleg/S, (tl) AridOcean/S, (tr) yamix/S, (tr) Gentoo Multimedia Ltd/S; 126–7 Doug Perrine/NPL, (bc) Barcroft Media/GI, (tc) Barcroft Media/GI; 126(l) funnyboy745/S, (tl) MarFot/S; 127(cr) Stuart Westmorland/CO, (tl) photo market/S, (tr) Doug Perrine/NPL; 128–9 Lorraine Swanson/S; 128(b) Wild Wonders of Europe/Radisic/NPL, (b) Matt Jeppson/S, (bl) Picsfive/S, (t) Rusty Dodson/S, (tl) Vasilius/S, (tr) Thomas Bethge/S; 129(b) David Thorpe/AL, (cr) Mitsuhiko Imamori/Minden Pictures/FLPA,

(tr) Fedorov Oleksiy/S, (tr) rsooll/S; 130–1 Yva Momatiuk & John Eastcott/Minden Pictures/FLPA, (b) James Steidl/S, (b) max blain/S, (t) James Steidl/S; 130(bl) Robert Dowling/CO, (cl) Jakub Krechowicz/S, (tl) Polina Maltseva/S; 131(bl) Roy Mangersnes/NPL, (bl) discpicture/S, (br) Jordi Bas Casas/PS, (tl) Michael & Patricia Fogden/CO, (tr) Mogens Trolle/S; 132–3 Michel & Christine Denis-Huot/GI; 132(bl) mashe/S, (l) Nigel Pavitt/JAI/CO, (l) Color Symphony/S, (tl) Willee Cole/S; 133(bc) Kevin George/S, (br) Elliott Neep/FLPA, (tr) Image Focus/S, (tr) Olga Makhanova/S; 134–5 David Gilder/S, (bc) Hunor Focze/S, (bc) Noah Golan/S; 134(bl) Solvin Zankl/Visuals Unlimited/CO, (bl) Katrina Brown/S, (tl) Michael Durham/Minden Pictures/FLPA, (tl) Michael Durham/Minden Pictures/FLPA, (tr) Joel Sartore/GI; 135(br) STR/Reuters/CO, (br) Eric Isselée/S, (tc) Daryl Balfou/GI, (tc) Johan Swanepoel/S; 136–7 Ingo Arndt/Minden Pictures/FLPA, (c) Hiroya Minakuchi/Minden Pictures/FLPA, (b) Doug Perrine/NPL; 136(c) Georgette Douwma/NPL, (c) Augusto Cabral/S, (tl) lafoto/S; 137(bl) NatalieJean/S, (tr) Sylvain Cordier/GI; 138–9 Mark Bolton/S; 138(c) Roger Powell/NPL, (b) Blackbirds/S, (cl) Robyn Mackenzie/S, (tl) Laborant/S, (tr) photocell/S; 139(bl) brandonht/S, (br) Gail Johnson/S, (br) Bytedust/S, (c) shutswis/S, (cl) Timothy W. Stone/S, (cl) Vitaly Korovin/S, (tl) Yuri Shirokov/S, (tr) Frans Lanting/FLPA; 140–1 Alena Brozova/S; 140(tl) Olivier Le Moal/S, (bl) Frans Lanting/CO, (r) RF, (tl) Valentin Agapov/S; 141(bl) Brigitte Thomas/GI, (br) Pete Oxford/Minden Pictures/FLPA, (br) crystalfoto/S, (cr) nito/S, (tc) Brooke Becker/S, (tl) Justine Evans/NPL; 142–3 Feng Yu/S, Tungphoto/S; 142(cl) ducu59us/S, (bl) Bruce Davidson/NPL, (bl) Brian A Jackson/S, (bl) PhotoHappiness/S, (br) Hal_P/S, (br) Ingvar Bjork/S, (cl) Anneka/S, (cr) Photo Researchers/FLPA, (tr) tanatat/S; 143(c) Kess/S, (br) Alex Hyde/NPL, (br) Mushakesa/S, (cl) GI, (cr) Ben Bryant/S, (tr) Winfried Wisniewski/FN/ Minden/FLPA; 144–5(tc) Mogens Trolle/S, donatas15/S, (c) Gavin Parsons/GI, (b) ImageBroker/FLPA; 144(b) Barbara Magnuson/Larry Kimball/GI, (c) Andy Rouse/NPL, (cl) bioraven/S, (l) Mazzzur/S, (tl) oriori/S, (tl) cloki/S; 145(br) Dickie Duckett/FLPA, (cr) MarkMirror/S, (r) Picsfive/S, (tr) Aditya Singh/Imagebroker/FLPA; 146–7 Michio Hoshino/Minden Pictures/FLPA; 146(bl) TungCheung/S, (br) Michio Hoshino/Minden Pictures/FLPA, (tl) Valentin Agapov/S, (tl) kzww/S, (tr) morrbyte/S; 147(bl) Dmitriy Bryndin/S, (br) Joel Sartore/GI, (tl) Rob Crandall/RF, (tr) Le Do/S; 148–9 Michael Poliza/GI; 148(bl) Dr. John Michael Fay/GI, (bl) Lukiyanova Natalia/frenta/S, (cl) 3d brained/S, (l) Nihongo/S, (tr) Leshik/S; 149(b) Barcroft Media/GI, (b) Selena/S, (tr) Ulrich Doering/Imagebroker/FLPA

150 rattanapatphoto/S

All other photographs are from: Corel, digitalSTOCK, digitalvision, Dreamstime.com, Fotolia.com, iStockphoto.com, John Foxx, PhotoAlto, PhotoDisc, PhotoEssentials, PhotoPro, Stockbyte

Every effort has been made to acknowledge the source and copyright holder of each picture. The publishers apologize for any unintentional errors or omissions.